STYLE FILE™
KNOW-HOW

By
Shelley Brown-Williams

TRAFFORD

Note for Librarians: a cataloguing record for this book that includes Dewey Classification and US Library of Congress numbers is available from the National Library of Canada. The complete cataloguing record can be obtained from the National Library's online database at: www.nlc-bnc.ca/amicus/index-e.html
ISBN 1-4120-1266-x

This book was published *on-demand* in cooperation with Trafford Publishing.
On-demand publishing is a unique process and service of making a book available for retail sale to the public taking advantage of on-demand manufacturing and Internet marketing. **On-demand publishing** includes promotions, retail sales, manufacturing, order fulfilment, accounting and collecting royalties on behalf of the author.

Suite 6E, 2333 Government St., Victoria, B.C. V8T 4P4, CANADA

Phone	250-383-6864	Toll-free	1-888-232-4444 (Canada & US)
Fax	250-383-6804	E-mail	sales@trafford.com
Web site	www.trafford.com	TRAFFORD PUBLISHING IS A DIVISION OF TRAFFORD HOLDINGS LTD.	
Trafford Catalogue #03-1644		www.trafford.com/robots/03-1644.html	

10   9   8   7   6   5   4   3   2

This book is dedicated
to all those
who encourage others.
Those who do so genuinely,
often with only a kind word or two,
empower others
to be all they can be.
What a priceless gift!

Jennifer,

Express your style —
always!

Shelly Brown-Williams

Acknowledgements

Writing a book gives you permission to share your essence with the world. It is never a single endeavour.

Thank you to my husband, Dave, not only for his love, but kindness, compassion and sense of humour – one does not often get such a second chance in life.

To my late husband, Graham who will always be with me.

To Cathy and Darlene – true best friends.

To the many girlfriends who have shared the enthusiasm of the Style File™; you have made this book a reality!

To my business manager, Jennifer, and artist/editor Caren. To editor and wonderful friend Lee. Circumstances bring amazing people into a life – thank you for your expertise and for who you are.

To the Style File™ Know-How models.

Models' hairstyles courtesy of Tony Sabine, Styles by Sabine – Victoria, BC.

Photography courtesy of Rebecca Kirstein, Studio One Photographic Arts – Sidney, BC.

Illustrations by Caren Riegel, artist, Victoria, BC.

Preface

"Fashion is a way of not having to decide who you are. Style is deciding who you are & being able to perpetuate it."

Quentin Crisp 1908 – 1999

Twenty years ago I started this business…on a dare! A friend was taking a colour/image consulting course and thought I should take it along with her. It was *so* much money, and my husband Graham (never knowing what I was up to next) tried very hard to be enthusiastic. I made him a deal: if this did not work out, I would return to work full time at the bank for as long as it took to pay off the business loan. It was a decision that changed my life forever.

I began with a home-based studio analyzing women's colours and doing their make-up. I *loved* when a client took the final look in the mirror and that "I-like-what-I-see" glow would radiate all over her face.

Soon after, a department store hired me as the fashion consultant and the position led to many different opportunities. That tenure expanded into creating fashion shows, business seminars, choosing clothing for corporations and events, dressing on-air personalities and, my most favorite, dressing women of all ages, sizes and lifestyles.

In the early 90s I was asked to create and teach curriculum for an image consulting school. It was there the new colour system was designed. When I completed teaching the course, I could think of nothing else but this colour system and how the students understood it so well. I gave up my full time job and spent the next six months putting Current Colours™ together. The following year, as I was about to launch Current Colours™, that tiny voice (that speaks so loudly in your head) said, "why would you stop at colours? Why can't women have all their fashion information?" Back to the drawing board and after several months The Style File™ Image Consulting System Inc. was born.

Shortly after opening, I had a new client come to have her Style File™ done. She was extremely shy and I soon realized how nervous she was! It didn't take too long for her to feel comfortable and understand that this was about to be a positive experience. But how was she to know that in advance? That day, I *got* what a privilege it was for me to help a woman discover her personal style.

Now, this proven, positive system needs to be shared with every woman. Yes, the Style File™ will teach you how to put it all together, but your new attitude and confidence will let the world know *"you've got style!"*

Shelley Brown-Williams
Victoria, BC, September 2003

A Style File™ Consultation

After an individual Style File™ consultation women receive their personal "style" in a "file". From colour and make-up shades, to lifestyles and proportions, the Style File™ wallet houses all their fashion information.

Table of Contents

Final Frontier

Final Frontier??? Save that for space. A woman's style should be her *ultimate* frontier.

Personal style is the visible expression of our inner essence. It's the magic that renders our smiles; the charisma that shapes our strut and shows the universe what we are all about. It has the ability to communicate our mood and mindset with the blink of an eye.

Style can appear classy or careless, fun or frumpy, sexy or sloppy, but one thing is for certain: we *all* come with style. It may or may not be what you truly would like to portray, but your style is as personal as your signature and you own them both!

We've come a long way baby, but…when it comes to this style thing – we're still lost in space. Any basic, common sense or *learned* knowledge is simply nowhere to be found!

Developing your style is actually a skill. Some may have been blessed with that innate, creative talent to state their nuance. But most of us need to go where few women have gone before, to learn the mode and manner of putting the puzzle pieces together. What a concept!

We learn just about every other task in life from math to computers, but this illusive thing called "style" is left mostly to trial and error. And we know what happens with those methods. The trials become frustrating and the errors too costly. End result: sticking to the tried, boring and true; same old, same old. Never boldly going where we give ourselves permission to express the outrageous, sensuous, elegant or trendy phases of our lives. So let's put some sense into our style and get that sassy little attitude thing happening.

Pardon? You would *like* to but it is really not for you? Of course it is. Let me ask you a question.

Have you ever been to a special occasion or certain event and found just the perfect outfit to wear? Oh my *gawd*. You just can't wait for the day. You look dynamite in this thing. The big day arrives, and you're a primpin'! Make-up is on, hair is just right, and now the outfit – hotdam the mirror is smokin'!

Guess what happens? By the time you arrive at your special event, you never think about how you look for the rest of the evening. It was handled before you left the house and now you are free to be you, to enjoy the occasion at hand.

Most of us know what happens when we do not handle our appearance. We sit through a miserable evening thinking how great everyone else looks. "I can't take my jacket off, my dress is too tight." "She looks so good with that hairstyle." "I wish I had put on my make-up." Sound familiar? Self punishment! We are experts at that.

Let's take this scenario one step further. Why would you wait for a special occasion, perhaps only a few times a year, to look your best? Every day is a special occasion and you deserve that *hotdam* attitude each time you glance in the mirror.

OK, you're conceding. You *do* want to look fabulous. If only you had the time and money for all this…

Good news. The Style File™ Image Consulting System Inc. will put you together with fun and flair, while saving you time and money. Its common sense approach will have you amazed at the simplicity of these easy ideas. You will look, feel and be *mah*-velous.

We are going to begin our quest with a short quiz to test your style smartz. Remember, although this may be slightly painful, honesty is not only the best policy, it will actually help you to see the error of the womanly way and get this style, image, good grooming, fashion thing working!

OK, here's how to score the quiz. You earn a point for each "no" answer for questions 1 through 7 and a point for each "yes" answer for questions 8 through 12. It's that easy!

Remember, h o n e s t answers are the only ones that work.

Stylefile™ Smartz (begsoata)

	Yes	No
Do you suffer from "sale syndrome" (a nasty, psychological disorder that causes one to purchase something just because it's on sale)?	Yes	No
Do you refuse to pay full price for your clothing?	Yes	No
Do you find yourself panic shopping (thinking you do not need a new article of clothing for an upcoming event and then at the last minute, deciding you do)?	Yes	No
Do you purchase clothing that doesn't quite fit hoping to lose those last few pounds?	Yes	No
Do you deprive yourself of new clothing until you lose weight?	Yes	No
Are you still wearing the same styles you did five years ago?	Yes	No
Do you have any "mistakes" hanging in your closet?	Yes	No
Do you know the correct alterations your body type requires?	Yes	No
Have you thoroughly cleaned your closet within the last year?	Yes	No
Do you know how to take advantage of all the new colours that are introduced each spring and fall for the coming fashion season?	Yes	No
Are you confident the clothing you purchase suits your style and body line?	Yes	No
Do you know the latest make-up tips and techniques?	Yes	No

If you scored between:

⅄ 11-12   You have a great sense of your personal style

⅄ 9-10   You are on the right track

⅄ < 8   Read, reread and read again; you're gonna love this book!

Oh, by the way did you happen to notice the word beside the title? (begsoata). Any good at unscrambling? The word is "sabotage" which is exactly what we, believe it or not, have been trained to do when we shop, dress or attempt to get-it-together! Hey, it's out with the old and in with the new Style File™.

Ready?

Set?

You go girl!

The Many Phases Of Eve

It's the morning routine: tumble out of bed, put on the coffee, and stand under the shower jets hoping to wake up. Betcha I know what you are thinking! "What am I going to wear today?" The closet doors open – if only something great would just jump out and jump on (clothing, that is) and solve the dilemma.

Oh, no doubt you have a few great pieces. There is the designer black skirt still hanging with the tags on (you'll wear it soon; you're working on losing those last few pounds), a purple tank that just needs something to go over it, classy navy pants (must get them hemmed), yada, yada, yada.

Do I dare say it: "A closet full of clothes and nothing to wear!" You are a most incredible example of the female species if you have never thought or uttered this comment before. How does this phenomenon happen? We will answer most of these strange questions in our closet-cleaning chapter, **Clutterless**, but you will be pleased to discover there is a missing ingredient each closet desperately needs.

The missing ingredient: determining your Clothing Lifestyle(s), for the here and now. This allows you to create a wardrobe that works. Gone are the days when you were categorized as a classic, romantic, dramatic, trendy, sporty – bor-r-ring. How old-fashioned is that? You have occasions to be all of those in your life.

For some, romantic can mean pretty and pink, for others it can mean black and beautiful. You may feel sporty in jeans and a crisp white shirt, while your best friend loves a big sweater over tights. Classic may be a tailored skirted suit, but your colleague may prefer a trendy, cropped pantsuit.

So the last century concepts stay there. And did I mention, so does the term classic? Classy is the new motto – tailored or trendy – classy speaks pizzazz.

To have a wardrobe that works for you, your clothes need to reflect your daily activities.

The good news is, as you evolve into each new stage of your life your clothing transforms with you. The clothing you wore five years ago is, or should be, outdated. Chances are your clothing needs and styles will differ again, a couple of years from now.

You may retire from an executive position and have a closet full of suits. Hang on to one or two, because a suit is a staple in any wardrobe, but what is the point of keeping them all?

C'mon Eve, I want you to really think about this. You can try and give me a reason your closet reveals your life history, but for every reason, I will give you a rebuttal (and a referral to the **Clutterless** chapter).

Oh? Would some of your reasons be…

I spent so much money on my suits.

Good, I bet you were polished and professional in your corporate days. Since you have retired, your occasions for suits are few and far between. Certainly keep one or two, but imagine how grateful a single, working mom would be, purchasing your suits at a second-hand store.

I won't have anything to wear.

You are not wearing most of the clothes in your closet anyways; why hang on to mistakes that are creating confusion and clutter?

I might need them some day.

Define "some day". By the time your "some day" comes around, chances are your clothes will be out of style.

The following chart will allow you to list your day-to-day, week-to-week commitments for the next month, and sensibly examine your wardrobe needs. Career, kids, classes, clubs, gym – any or all of the above.

		Career	Hobbies, Clubs	Activities
Week 1	**Sunday**			
	Monday			
	Tuesday			
	Wednesday			
	Thursday			shopping
	Friday			
	Saturday			
Week 2	**Sunday**			
	Monday			
	Tuesday			
	Wednesday			
	Thursday			
	Friday			
	Saturday			
Week 3	**Sunday**			
	Monday			
	Tuesday			
	Wednesday			
	Thursday			
	Friday			
	Saturday			
Week 4	**Sunday**			
	Monday			
	Tuesday			
	Wednesday			
	Thursday			
	Friday			
	Saturday			

Exercise	Social	Classes	Travel
tennis.			

Another dated notion was a generic list of what a basic wardrobe should include. According to whom? Each of us differs in our choice of lifestyles, careers, and interests (not to mention our shapes). How can we possibly give a one-list-fits-all?

Enter The Style File's™ *Clothing Lifestyles* – a refreshing new approach to determine your current wardrobe needs. No more plunking you in a category and leaving you there. This system changes along with the many phases of your life. Well, that is too darn easy!

Let's look at the five Clothing Lifestyles and see which one(s) fit into your current regime. Most women have a "business" lifestyle and a "casual" lifestyle. For some, the two may intertwine. There is no right or wrong – just what works for you.

Metropolitan

A Metropolitan lifestyle is predominately suited to the corporate world. Ms. Metropolitan usually handles her business wardrobe with

discipline and diligence. She knows the power of a positive image and harnesses that confidence to her advantage. She is very comfortable with her professional, chic and *classy* look.

Ms. Metropolitan no longer feels she must emulate the navy-blazer-gray-skirt costume that catapulted her into a man's world several decades ago. Classic has graduated to classy, with suits in a variety of fabrics, styles and colours to complement the individual and her taste. Ms. Metropolitan is comfortable in her business attire because, more often than not, she is a highly organized and efficient person. Reflecting on the outside what you are all about on the inside exposes a harmonious, happy woman.

A note for Ms. Metro: *Never under-estimate the power of your suit!* The dynamic presence that a well-fitting skirt or pantsuit exudes is an influential tool the wise businesswoman does not leave home without.

A few years ago, a magazine article printed a psychological experiment done in the workplace. Two executives, one male and one female, were to visit various offices as the "boss" and "executive assistant". Both were dressed in suits. Staff members were polled after as to who was who. Not too bad for the women - 40% believed the female was the boss while 60% believed the male was in charge, a large improvement from decades before. Then came the crunch; both were asked to remove their jackets and repeat the exercise.

Can you guess the results? Most chose the male as the "boss" and the female as the "executive assistant". The power of a blazer governs an unwritten rule in the competitive game of business. Those who choose to learn and master the rules of the game win – and our motivated, Ms. Metropolitan loves to win!

Westcoast

Whether business or pleasure, 70% of women will incorporate the Westcoast lifestyle into their wardrobe plan. Westcoast is not a location, rather an attitude. Key words describing this Clothing Lifestyle are "casually smart" or "casually elegant". Westcoast women have a unique, often subtle flair to their contemporary look.

Westcoast is appropriate for many occasions. Although less formal than Metropolitan, the Westcoast lifestyle suits many professions. Some may call it "business casual" or as we have mentioned, "casually smart". The look may *appear* more relaxed, but it is always put together and well coordinated. Ms. Westcoast never sells herself short. She knows the negative connotations of appearing too casual when she means business; even the slightest of details are carefully handled.

(Business casual is the *only* acceptable look for casual Fridays – a day that has become the downfall to the image and reputation of employers and employees.)

Often, Westcoast is the "off hours" look for Ms. Metropolitan. This is as casual as it gets for her. Volunteering, meetings, school functions, you name it – Westcoast fits many women's clothing requirements.

Uptown

♬ Uptown girl ♬ … ♬ Livin' in her uptown world. ♬

Wouldn't we *all* love to be uptown! Creative, trendy, artsy – that is what she is all about. Mizz Uptown can put the most outrageous pieces together and look fabulous, the rest of us… we just don't go there. Mz. Uptown *loves* new styles and bores easily with the old. While most women are j-u-s-t beginning to visually adapt to a new fad or fashion, Mz. Uptown has ventured on to hot-off-the-runway's latest craze. She has fun with fashion, while using her unusual look to provoke a sassy sense of confidence.

We all know Uptown women. Among them are artists, potters, hairstylists, media types and innovative inventors with an insatiable appetite to create.

Mixing patterns, textures and different colour combinations comes naturally for this lifestyle. The "norm" is simply too basic. Put an Uptown in a tailored business suit and you may as well be putting her in a straight jacket!

Just like an Uptown's clothing, hairstyles and make-up mirror up-to-the-minute fashion. Whether her hair is long, short, red or black (all in the same month) it will never remain the same for too long. Casual or career, Mz. Uptown is uptown through and through.

Cosmopolitan

Miss Cosmopolitan is the epitome of femininity. She loves being a woman and has usually been blessed with a curvy silhouette and soft features including full lips.

She is most comfortable in clothing with movement – dresses, skirts and drapey trousers. She favors fabrics patterned with polka dots, prints and florals. Capes, strappy heels, mules, glitzy jewellery, strands of pearls; a Cosmo girl will always complete her outfits with perfectly pretty accessories. Her hairstyles are longer and softer, never short or severe. Rarely without make-up, her full lips are stained to perfection and nails well manicured with bright shades of polish.

Her clothing dilemma is a closet full of her favorite after-five outfits. Looking for business clothing is always a challenge.

I met a most memorable Cosmo girl several years ago, when she hired me to help plan a business wardrobe. Our first appointment was at her home to start the process with a closet clean. I knocked on the door of her apartment and there she was – Miss Cosmopolitan. She had long, soft curly hair, dressed in tights with a long, floral sweater. We chatted for a bit and then went to her closet. Upon opening the doors, the most beautiful "garden" hung before me. There were floral dresses, polka dot slacks and sweaters embroidered with rosettes and scalloped edges. No wonder she was having difficulty with a work wardrobe!

Every time she went shopping, another softly patterned garment was added to her closet. She couldn't resist!

Our Miss Cosmo had just been promoted to a supervisory position and knew her teatime wardrobe was not appropriate for the office. Her subconscious Cosmopolitan programming equated work attire with a masculine, way-too-tailored look.

After learning that suits came in a variety of beautiful fabrics, shapes and colours, our femme fatale realized she had a variety of styles to choose from. Whew!

Suburban

Suburban's motto is, or should be, *casually coordinated*. Every pair of female eyes reading this book has a slice of Suburban in her life. Ms. Suburban's biggest complaint (or bluntly put, bad habit) is casual becomes too casual and her look *and* outlook deteriorates rapidly from there.

Do any of the following "suburbanizers" fit into your regime? If so, tick the appropriate box:

☐ My weekend wear

☐ Off hours from my full time job

☐ I have a home-based business

☐ I am retired

☐ The mom syndrome

Far from the "oh-well-it-doesn't-matter" casual look of sweats and tees, Suburban has great style. Think about this, if you were employed outside the home, you would have suitable work wear, correct? Well, if Suburban is *part* or *all* of your present lifestyle, why would you not allow yourself at least a couple of up-to-date casual outfits? Really, why not?

Ms. Suburban keeps her casual, casual. Jackets, loafers and totes keep in line with the relaxed theme. No mixing business blouses with khaki cottons or jeans. Her inspiring combinations leave one with the impression she *always* looks good. Before you check out some Suburban basics in the **Essentials** chapter, I want you to double check whether or not you are falling victim to any of the fashion faux pas listed below:

o   Bulky socks and old runners with your jeans

o   Tee shirts that are terribly tired (that is as politely as I can put it)

o   Poorly fitting slacks/jeans

o   Pilled sweaters

o   Tattered shoes

o   Your sister's or mom's old fashioned hand-me-downs

Not quite getting it? OK. This should do it. Would you send your children to school with any of the above afflictions? Not likely. Taking care of everyone else but yourself? Tsk, tsk.

Regardless of your current clothing lifestyles, always set the tone and the example. Personal style, whether casual or corporate, is healthy, positive and an outer expression that shows you care!

igure It Out

This may be the most difficult chapter for many women. And who can blame us. From every visual perspective, we are bombarded with what "beauty" should look like. Magazines, movies, billboards and, most recently, the Internet depict the gorgeous, ideal woman. On an intellectual level, we know how "doctored" the images are, but from our innermost desires to look beautiful, we don't care! We want to look like that!

Really? Think again. I want you to imagine the most beautiful-looking woman who comes to mind. Now, imagine every single female looked like that. You would do most anything and everything to be recognized for who you are! Well…nature has taken care of that for you; no one can be quite the same as you. Hey, it's in to be proud of who you are and your differences.

As far as beauty goes, let's take a look at what the dictionary has to say.

- Beauty: qualities that give pleasure to the senses or exalt the mind
- Beautify: to make or grow beautiful
- Beautiful: characterized by beauty

Figure it out…people are not born beautiful, their inner essence develops *qualities,* as they *grow* beautiful. True beauty maximizes all our plusses with a positive attitude. The result: a magnetic attraction of a confident one-of-a-kind.

Well, this is exciting – let's maximize! Where do we start? Several years ago I read a sentence in a book that has stuck with me since: "we dress bodies we know little about". How true! We can easily spot someone else's fashion faux pas, but when it comes to looking at our own reflection, the cloud of emotion blurs any possible objectivity.

Those issues aside, have you ever actually taken the time to study your shape? Hmm…I am betting for the most part, the answer is "no".

Here we go! If you are not complaining about a certain feature – it is a positive. We are so quick to point out the few things we do not like about ourselves; we fail to recognize our plusses.

Isn't it interesting that when a loved one or close friend is feeling down, we are happy to encourage them and reaffirm their many qualities? How about doing the same with your friend in the mirror?

So…take a deep breath, do the posture exercise (see **Puttin' on the Ritz** chapter) and let's tackle this.

Before you begin the assessment in front of a full-length mirror, proper attire is a must. Whether a bathing suit, bodysuit or your birthday suit, your silhouette needs to be as bare as possible.

Please remember, putting it all together is much like finding the right puzzle pieces to complete the picture. While we are about to describe *general* silhouettes and proportions (s/p), the combinations vary from woman to woman. It is up to each woman to choose the correct pieces of s/p to complete her individual picture.

Silhouette – "the outer contour of an object."

Our outer contour is where we begin. Your silhouette is determined by the proportion of your shoulders to the proportion of your hips. Stand facing the mirror.

- o Is the outside of your shoulders broader than the outside of your hips?
- o Is the outside of your shoulders even with the outside of your hips?
- o Is the outside of your shoulders narrower than the outside of your hips?

Simply choose the appropriate silhouette:

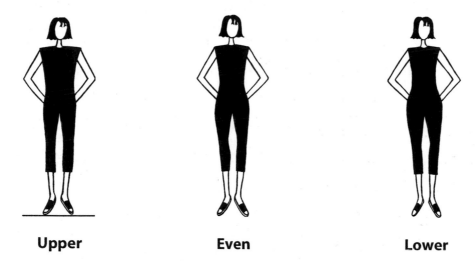

Upper   **Even**   **Lower**

Knowing your silhouette begins the process to help you understand why you choose or avoid certain styles. For example:

Upper Silhouettes
- Broad, athletic shoulders
- Typically a thicker waist
- Narrow hips and often a flatter derriere

(All uppers have broad shoulders but not necessarily the other particulars just mentioned.)

Upper silhouettes should:

- Remove shoulder pads
- Avoid boat necklines
- Choose raglan or set-in sleeves

o Avoid boxy styles

o Avoid stiff and/or bulky fabrics

Even Silhouettes

o Shoulder-to-hip proportions fairly even

o Attention given to individual proportions

o Many variables from one even silhouette to another

Even silhouettes should:

o Choose shoulder pads if shoulders slope

o Avoid shoulder pads if shoulders are square

We could go over every proportion and do the same comparison for an even silhouette, but it is more sensible to refer to the Proportion Profile following the silhouettes.

Lower Silhouettes

o 65%-70% of women fall into this category

o Curvy, with a significant difference between waist and hip measurement

o Often short waisted

Lower silhouettes should:

o Choose a small, rounded shoulder pad

o Use the alteration of taking in waist

o Take into account they are a smaller size on top

o Choose narrow or no waistbands

Yes, you are genetically disposed, but exercise and a little weight training can broaden the shoulders and alter your silhouette.

The Puzzle Pieces

Knowing your Proportion Profile removes the guesswork from shopping and eliminates costly mistakes. You must be honest and objective in determining your personal shape. What you are about to discover is that your Proportion Profile confirms many of the clothing choices you instinctively make – now you will know why. Be certain to take each of the puzzle pieces into account as you stylize your figure. Remember that each woman's combinations are different. Circle your individual proportions or write them in the margin while you stand in front of the mirror and visually get to know your body. Once you have honestly analyzed your silhouette and proportions, the following Style File™ Know-How should help to put you together.

Proportion Profile

Neckline (Length)

Short	Long
❖ wear collars open	❖ choose mock, turtle, funnel
❖ choose blouses, not shirts	❖ wear collars open or closed
❖ choose V, U, scoop, square	❖ choose cotton shirts
❖ avoid shoulder pads and stiff fabrics	❖ choose jewel or crew neck
❖ avoid high jewel/crew necks	❖ choose stand up or mandarin collars
❖ choose open placket or lowered collars	❖ choose shirt style, open placket blouses

stylefile smartz • If you do not know whether you are long or short in the neck, chances are you are medium length and necklines are not a big issue for you. Glean from other proportions what works best for you.

Shoulders

Broad	Narrow	Sloped
❖ avoid shoulder pads	❖ choose shoulder pads	❖ always wear shoulder pads
❖ avoid bulky, heavy fabrics	❖ choose set-in sleeves	❖ choose set-in sleeve
❖ choose set-in sleeves	❖ choose slightly dropped sleeve	❖ avoid raglan
❖ choose raglan sleeves	❖ avoid raglan sleeves	❖ choose horizontal detail at shoulders
❖ choose halter necklines	❖ choose detail at shoulder level	
❖ avoid horizontal detail at shoulder level		

Bust Line

Small	Full
❖ choose crew, jewel necks	❖ choose simple, clean lines for tops
❖ avoid tight, clinging knits	❖ choose fine knits
❖ choose mocks, turtlenecks	❖ choose blazers with no lapels/V/ scoop necklines
❖ select blazers with lapels	❖ choose open placket blouses
❖ choose tops with detail – piping, pockets, crests	❖ look for fitted bodice; avoid boxy styles
	❖ choose smooth, drapable fabrics

Arms

Short	Long
❖ ensure long sleeves are hemmed to correct length	❖ ensure long sleeves are lengthened to correct length
❖ choose short sleeves	❖ favorite length–¾ sleeve or push up sleeves
❖ avoid above-elbow, short sleeve	❖ choose short or above-elbow short sleeve

stylefile smartz • With a little workout, you too can wear sleeveless. Arms respond quickly to weight training.

Rise/Tummy

Short Rise, Flat Tummy	Long Rise, Round Tummy
❖ choose side closure slacks	❖ choose fly front
❖ select flat front or darts	❖ select pleated slacks
❖ select in seam pockets	❖ select slash pockets

Waistline

Short-Waisted	Long-Waisted
❖ choose "no waistband" or narrow waistbands	❖ choose medium to wider waistbands/ belts
❖ narrow belts to coordinate with top	❖ belts to tone with slacks/ skirts
❖ slightly "blouson" tucked in tops	❖ avoid skinny tops
❖ choose hip length blouses/sweaters	❖ avoid short, cropped jackets
❖ choose smooth, drapable fabrics	❖ choose medium-longer length jackets/blazers

Hips

Narrow	Full
❖ fit through waist, take in at hips	❖ fit through hip, take in at waist
❖ choose flat front slacks	❖ choose hip-medium length blazers/ jackets
❖ choose two-piece dressing	❖ choose smooth, drapable fabrics
❖ avoid flowy fabrics	❖ look for cutaway front, side vents in jackets

Legs

Short	Long
❖ choose slim-medium pant leg width	❖ choose medium-wider leg pant
❖ shoes and hose to blend/coordinate	❖ hem long skirts 6"-7" from floor
❖ hem long skirts 7" from floor	❖ choose different colour tops and bottoms

Fabrics

Slim Silhouette	Curvy Silhouette
❖ avoid flimsy or voluminous fabrics	❖ avoid bulky fabrics
❖ choose textures with substance	❖ look for smooth, drapable fabrics that work with your curves

If you have carefully read through the various proportions and determined what works best for you, I would like you to go to your closet. Look at your favorite pieces. Not only does the colour and style personally suit you, but all the details that flatter your proportions can be checked off accordingly. For example if you have a short neck, your V or U shape sweater will be lovingly worn out, while the turtleneck sits on the shelf; a sloping shoulder chooses a soft, rounded shoulder pad (even when they are not in style) to create the illusion of a more balanced figure; a long waisted woman prefers a waistband and a medium to wider width belt to proportion her torso. For every "favorite" or "mistake" there is a reason why.

This all-important chapter is worth the extra time it takes in order to visually understand your silhouette and proportions. The woman with style is uncompromising when selecting flattering lines, colours and fit. Personal style develops when you know what, why and how to choose your clothing.

Analyze a favorite item and learn to identify each feature that is personally becoming. Scrutinize your mistakes as well to avoid repeating them in the future. Your mistakes could be someone else's favorites. Part with them and find them a good home!

How Fitting

If this book does nothing else but give you permission to alter your clothing, it will have accomplished a great feat!

Scenario #1

Mr. Smith is purchasing a suit. The salesperson calls the tailor to do some adjustments. "Mr. Smith, would you like your trousers with or without a cuff?"

"With a cuff," Mr. Smith replies.

"I see you have one shoulder lower than the other. We will put in an extra shoulder pad and take in the back seam for a better fit," the tailor says.

(Mr. Smith could care less if one shoulder is lower than the other.)

"Good, fine, when do I pick it up?" asks Mr. Smith.

Scenario #2

Mrs. Smith needs a suit. She has tried on soooo many and none of them seem to work for her. Finally, she puts on a beautiful berry suit. It hangs so nicely and it fits everywhere, but is too big in the waist. (Sound familiar?) The salesperson calls the seamstress.

"Mrs. Smith, all we need to do is take in the waist and it will fit you perfectly!"

What does Mrs. Smith say? Oh, about the same old thing that 90% of all women say.

"W e l l…I think I'm going to look around; thanks anyway."

Mrs. Smith gets dressed and carries on to the next store.

Now she is into punishment mode. "I hate my body; nothing works; nothing fits." The self-destructive tape is in full play. "I am not paying for alterations; men get theirs for free."

OK.

STOP THE TAPE!!!

Admit it, how many of you have uttered those comments?

This chapter brings such a common sense approach to choosing your wardrobe you will wonder why something so straightforward has been so neglected.

Very simply – clothing comes in standard sizing; our bodies do not.

Ninety percent of women need alterations. Using the excuse that men's alterations are covered and we have to pay still doesn't change reality. You still need alterations to ensure a good fit!

Besides, in better men and women's clothing stores, basic alterations are often covered. In other stores, men and women have to pay the nominal charge for an adjustment.

To miss out on a beautiful outfit because you will not pay the $15 or $20 on alterations is totally unreasonable. The woman who owns her style knows precisely what areas need tending to and never compromises on fit.

Most women look after hemming their slacks.

Let us look at some other necessary alterations:

Hemming sleeves

Always hem sleeves to the correct length. It does not matter whether you need to hem your sleeves ½" or 3". Be particular. Sloppy sleeves that are too long look like you are wearing someone else's clothing. Often tightening the button on a cuff is all you need to do. However, if the sleeve is so long it hangs over the cuff, you are creating excessive fullness. And, what part of your body do your wrists line up with? Your hips! Not a good idea to add bulk in that area! The seamstress removes the cuff and shortens the sleeve length. A neat sleeve that fits well is a must!

Wrists and ankles are "skinny bits" – don't hide them!

Narrowing the shoulders for smaller top sizes

Lower silhouettes are a smaller size on the top. If there is more than a two-size differential between your top and bottom, choosing blazers and jackets can be an issue. If the blazer fits through the shoulders, it can be too small through the hips. When you try on a larger size that fits the hips, the shoulders are too big. The seamstress narrows the shoulder seam of the blazer to correctly fit your shoulders.

stylefile smartz • If the shoulders fit well, but the jacket d o e s n ' t q u i t e do up, don't worry. Most one or two button blazers are never done up anyway, as the look is too stiff. Go with the size that fits you in the shoulders.

Taking in the waistband for fuller hips

This is an essential alteration for so many women. Most "lower" silhouettes struggle to find slacks that fit. If they fit through the hips, they are usually too big in the waist. When you choose a smaller size to snug up the waist, the fabric pulls through the hips. Grrr!

stylefile smartz • **Always fit through the fuller proportion and take in where necessary. Fit the hips properly and allow the seamstress to take in the waist.**

Taking in the sides for narrow hips

If you are a standard "upper" silhouette, you are thicker through the waist and narrow in the hips. Follow common sense and fit the larger proportion. Fit your waist; then take in the sides. If you are narrow in the hip, you will be most comfortable in flat front slacks. Many flat front pants come without pockets allowing for a simpler alteration of taking in the sides.

Raising the stride for flatter derrieres

As well as narrow hips, upper silhouettes often have a flatter derriere. Finding pants that fit through the bottom becomes a frustrating effort. The excess material is unbecoming from the rear view. A seamstress removes the waistband and "lifts up" the extra material, known as "raising the stride", or shortens the rear through the crotch seam.

stylefile smartz • Look in the lingerie section for briefs that have a gathered seam up the middle. It puts new meaning to the term lift and separate! The added shape it provides looks terrific under slacks and straight skirts. Also, choose back detailing, such as pockets and yokes, to visually add shape to the rear view.

Taking up a blazer for full-figured petites

If you are a full-figured petite, you may find that petite jackets do not fit. You need a standard size for the bodice, but the length is often too long. If it does not interfere with patch pockets, consider having the length of the blazer taken up to fit your proportion.

stylefile smartz • Rest your arms at your side. A medium length blazer should rest in the cuff of your palms without bending your elbow or folding up the bottom hem of the blazer. Unless you have unusually long arms, the length reaching the cuff of your palm will put your standard blazer in proportion to your silhouette.

Skirt Lengths

Long skirts are for everyone

Do you put on a long skirt and feel overwhelmed? No matter how short or how tall you are, you *can* wear the longer length skirts. Standing in stocking feet, hem your skirt seven inches from the floor to the bottom of your hem. That is the magic measurement to put a long skirt in proportion to your height. If you are 5'8" or taller, you can decrease the distance from stocking feet to the skirt's hem to five or six inches.

Shorter skirts – know what is best for you

For those who can easily wear a short skirt above the knee, you probably do not need to worry about a precise length until you are many years down the road, but...one day... For the rest of us, "a word to the wise is sufficient"!

You can have a short skirt that is on the knee or just below the knee. The key to creating the illusion of a short skirt is *never* covering the top part of your calf. As soon as you do, the look becomes "matronly". Do I have your attention now?

Some silhouettes look boxy if they wear a skirt above the knee. For example, those with broad shoulders and/or a full bosom will only accentuate their shoulders and bust if they wear skirts above the knee. The extra few inches gained by hemming just below the knee, visually lengthens the silhouette.

Regardless of any alteration particular to your silhouette or proportion, you now have official permission to *just do it*! Your self-esteem and style will forever thank you!

 stylefile smartz • *Just a suggestion...for those of you who sew or have ever sewn, the idea of paying for your pants to be hemmed seems out of the question. So, the slacks stay in the "to do" pile, reminding you of yet another task to complete. Here's a thought. You only have so many hours in a day. If sewing is not one of your favorite jobs, give it to some one whose job it is! A win-win for both of you.*

Current Colours™

This is where it all began for me. Thank you Carole Jackson, author and creator of *Color Me Beautiful*, for waking up women (and men) to the fact that colour works!

Colour was one of the first tangible tools that women of the late 70's utilized to choose suitable clothing. Thinking in terms of "colours" had never occurred to most.

I will always remember my Mother allowing me to purchase my first coat as a teenager. Duffle coats were the rage, and I traipsed from store to store trying on the popular camel duffle coat. Somehow, it never "fit" quite properly. My last effort was at our downtown Hudson's Bay store, where a burgundy duffle coat stood out amongst the camel. I tried it on and it "fit"! I wore it for many fall/winters feeling great every time I put it on. I would not know for several years to come, it was the burgundy colour that made the duffle coat such a favorite.

While the original colour system worked on strict guidelines to help us understand how to determine our best colours, we have graduated to a flexible, updated system that allows us to express our individuality, while choosing *all* the hues and shades that are right for our colouring, characteristics and personality.

Introducing Current Colours™...

Current Colours™ is the exciting new system that "updates" your colours every fashion season (spring/summer and fall/winter). As new styles and shades are launched semi-annually, Style File™ and Current Colours™ clients return to have their colours updated. All their new colour swatches are put into their Style File™ wallet, while the outdated swatches are removed.

It is more than excitement that causes women to shop when they know their colours; it is the confidence gained saving valuable time, costly mistakes and finally putting wardrobe dollars to their best use. What a concept!

stylefile smartz • Special "art paper" swatches are used in the Current Colours™ system for a good reason. This encourages you to use your swatches as a guide, not trying to match material swatches to your potential purchases.

Twenty years ago, retailers were more than frustrated when we compared our material swatches to every item in the store! If it did not match exactly, many women would not consider trying the outfit on.

Think about this – I can have one "dye" and 10 assorted fabrics. Each fabric will absorb the dye differently, resulting in 10 various shades of that colour. Thus, we women of the 21st century wisely use swatches as a guide *only.*

If your Style File™ consultant were to give you a swatch of every single shade and colour that would suit you, you would carry around a catalogue!!! Each fashion season, Style File™ clients have anywhere from 20 to 30 art paper swatches in their palette. *Every* colour is correct for them *and* currently in fashion.

Colour Characteristics

Many women think in terms of warm and cool tones when it comes to choosing colours – that is partly correct.

Colour actually has six characteristics:

o   Warm & cool

o   Light & deep

o   Bright & muted

We have a combination of all six of those characteristics in our skin tone, not just the warm and cool attributes. These personal characteristics translate into hues and tones that naturally flatter us more than other shades.

Current Colours™ uses six general categories in determining a person's colours. One of the many features of Current Colours™ is the individual preparation of each palette. There can be 10 "Crystals" with 10 different "Crystal" palettes.

Let us look at the 6 categories.

Are you:

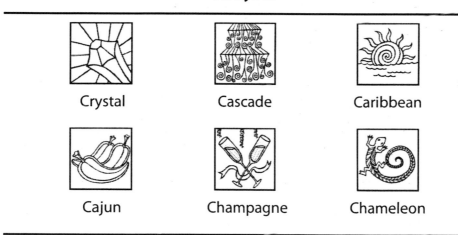

| Crystal | Cascade | Caribbean |
| Cajun | Champagne | Chameleon |

or a combination?

Here are the characteristics of each Current Colours™ category:

o   Crystal – cool, deep and bright

o   Cascade – cool, soft and light

o   Caribbean – warm, light and bright

o   Cajun – warm, deep and muted

o   Champagne – light and muted

o   Chameleon – deep and muted

The first four categories are *similar* to the "seasons" concept. The last two categories fill in some confusing gaps.

 Champagne

The first characteristic of a Champagne is not warm or cool, it is *light*. This person was often classed as a "summer", yet other seasonal consultants saw her as a "spring". In fact, both were somewhat right. She can wear dusty rose *or* soft peach. Her light neutral is winter white and/or cream. She looks elegant in beige, taupe and stone.

A Champagne needs light to medium *values* of colour, often with muted intensity. Her favorite fun tones are crossover colours – colours that are mixed with warm and cool hues such as coral, turquoise and periwinkle. These crossover colours suit many other categories as well.

Put a deep, dark colour on a Champagne and it looks "heavy". Champagne is the only category that does not successfully wear black. Almost everyone else *can* wear black.

 Chameleon

This category is the opposite of a Champagne. She may have been analyzed as a "winter" or an "autumn". Again both seasonal consultants would have been partially correct. Chameleons need depth (not to be confused with brightness) to their colours: charcoal gray, chocolate brown, indigo, eggplant, raisin – rich beautiful shades. They never wear pastels and their lighter shades are dusty or muted. Depending on individual characteristics, Chameleons will surprisingly wear a strong canary yellow and/or red. No category is exact. This is the beauty of the system: to make the very most of the person – not the category.

 Crystal

Crystals have a brightness to their look. They can wear clear, cool colours that are bold and lively. They feel crisp and clean wearing pure white and can wear icy tones and/or pastels.

Is it a coincidence that many crystals have bubbly, outgoing personalities? Absolutely not! Personalities play a big role in determining colour.

You can have two people with similar colouring:

    a. Quiet, reserved   b. Outgoing, adventurous

A bold fuchsia on person "a" will be overpowering, while flattering person "b" to a tee.

Remember, your colours are determined by your skin tone, hair, eyes *and* personality.

 Cascade

Colours that are cool and have a medium or normal value suit Cascades. If and when Cascades are tanned they often look good in pure white, but winter white looks good on them all year round. Cool pastels, berry tones, pine green and most blues are this category's favorites.

 Caribbean

Warm and bright, like its location, Caribbeans look so good in buttercup yellow, apple green, melon and poppy red. Their light neutral is cream, with lots of beige for wardrobe coordination. Often green or blue eyed, their warm-toned skin has golden, beige or peach tones.

Cajun

Think spicy – she's a hot tamale! The deep, warm tones of pumpkin, olive, mustard, and mahogany enhance a Cajun's skin tone. Lighter, warm shades are muted. This is the woman who would never wear a white wedding gown – her light neutral is cream or ivory. Contrary to original colour systems, Cajuns look fabulous in black.

Combination

Many women have a combination category. For example, a Crystal/Cascade has a cool base skin tone that can wear most any cool tone colour, light, bright or deep. A Caribbean/Champagne needs light colours leaning more toward the warmer tones. What would the first characteristic be for a Caribbean/Cajun? That's right – warm. This combination category can choose from a full range of warm-tone hues.

stylefile smartz • If you put on an incorrect colour you will find the eye looks at the colour, then travels up to your face; it will do this several times, trying to visually make the colour work. (It won't!) However, if the colour personally suits you, the eye is instantly drawn to the face for a pleasant, harmonious appearance.

Remember, no longer classed in one season, we can successfully choose colours that are personally flattering and currently in fashion.

Many women, who follow the rigidity of an old colour system to excess, will feel frustration and confusion hanging on to outdated methods. I want you to *read and reread* this section to undo some previous misconceptions. Open up the lid and jump out of the box. Knowing your Current Colours™ is a tool too valuable to waste.

Please keep in mind that "colours" had to begin somewhere. What an amazing feat to invent the application of personal colour and put it into such an easy system as "seasons". But, as in any area of learning and knowledge, the system grows and changes to accommodate new ideas and methods – Current Colours™ is the result of refurbishing such an incredible idea.

stylefile smartz • If you are looking in the mirror and thinking something is not quite right – chances are, it isn't, or you would not have asked yourself the question. On the other hand, if you think your outfit looks good, but are thinking inside the box that you are "not supposed" to be wearing that colour, think again. More often than not, you instinctively choose what naturally flatters you.

Let's examine some of the old colour "myths" and put them to bed.

Myth #1 Bare face and covered hair

When we first had our colours done some 25 years ago, we were analyzed without make-up and often with a white scarf over our hair.

Well, most of us wear make-up and do not walk around with our hair covered! If you choose correct make-up to naturally enhance your skin tone, wrong colours will still show through during colour analysis, but your better colours look fabulous! Remember, not only is your hair a huge part of your overall style, it too plays a part in harmoniously determining your colours.

Myth #2 Once and forever analyzed

You are always changing. This is a fact of life. And, along with the many changes in your life, let's not forget your skin tone changes as well. The variation in your skin tone will result in the variation of your clothing colours. You are *not* one colour category or "season" forever. The beauty of Current Colours™ updates is that it allows you to look your best at every age and stage in life.

stylefile smartz • The Neutral Zone. As people enter middle age, more often than not, their colours differ from shades and hues of their 20's and 30's. If you have generally worn intense, bright colours, they may suddenly feel too harsh. Pink shades of make-up often feel like they are "sitting" on the skin rather than blending and accentuating. The deep warm spicy tones may feel too heavy as your skin and hair are becoming lighter. Softer shades of clothing and make-up colours may now be more flattering. You are entering The Neutral Zone: a time to reinvent your colours in clothing, hair and make-up. The difference is nothing short of amazing. Style captures the grace and beauty of every stage of your life; knowing this particular time in your journey will never be the same again.

Myth #3 Only "winters" wear black

It was thought that only "winters" could wear black, simply not so. Black suits every category in the new Current Colours™ system except a Champagne. As mentioned, a Champagne's first characteristic is light. Black or very dark colours have too much depth and overwhelm the light Champagne features.

Occasionally, people who have light characteristics that equal their other traits *do* find black too dominant. Rest assured, black is a fabulous neutral for the majority of the population.

Myth#4 Hair colour

It was originally suggested that you should dye your hair with shades complimentary to your warm or cool skin tone. *So not true!* The 80s and 90s brought about the "red" revolution in hair colour and it was hot! Plain old auburn was just that – plain and old. Burgundy, mahogany and many other wonderful shades of red hair rinses, tints and dyes were introduced and we still cannot get enough of them. Hey, fashion is all about trends and keeping up-to-date, so if you choose a new colour for your hair, your clothing colours can easily be adjusted. Remember…think out of that box!

Myth #5 Cool tones wear silver; warm tones wear gold

Silver and gold-tone accessories are not a warm and cool issue, they are an intensity factor. Cool tone skin can wear gold successfully as long as it has a sheen; a matte or florentine gold will look dull on a cool, clear skin tone. The opposite works for warm-toned skin. Warm tones can wear all intensities of gold-tone, but when it comes to silver, they are more flattered by matte or pewter.

I know this "myth" section may be a tuffy for some of you, but please follow the suggestion of reading and rereading. Never get stuck in the past or as someone so blatantly put it, "don't be a time-warp-Tina"!

The tool of colour analysis is too important to overlook. Choosing your Current Colours™ will not only light a spark in your wardrobe, it will have you naturally glowing – all the time!

COLOUR IS FREE! Now you can take advantage of the biggest bonus your style and wardrobe can offer. You are going to love Current Colours.™

Meet some Style File™ clients; women just like you who have busy lives and like to look their best. Regardless of age, capturing each stage of your life with confidence and care reveals the beauty of personal style.

Nicole – As you look at Nicole's cool and bright colour characteristics, you can see clear strong colours from the Crystal category naturally flatter her. Nicole is a personal trainer and aerobics instructor. Her upper silhouette is typical of athletic physiques and Nicole's incredibly fit shape looks great in her Uptown choices of aerobic wear and casual wear. Balancing career, husband and two sons, Nicole's thirty-something energy is filled with a contagious zest for life.

Elizabeth – Elizabeth's colouring is warm, light and bright – all the characteristics of a Caribbean. She was fascinated to discover why she enjoyed the more feminine styles in clothing. As soon as the Clothing Lifestyle system was explained to her, she responded, "oh you mean Cosmopolitan is a girlie-girl; that's me!" Long hair, curvy even silhouette and the love for swishy, drapable styles are *so* Miss Cosmo. At 37, Elizabeth is a wife, mom, businesswoman with hair fashion pieces and is currently working on her masters.

Fern – Classy describes our Westcoast Fern. Muted, elegant shades compliment her light characteristics of Champagne leaning slightly toward a Champagne/Caribbean. With an even silhouette, Fern looks and feels right at home in casually smart or casually elegant styles. Fern is an expert seamstress who teaches sewing and specializes in pattern fitting. Whether keeping fit walking her dogs, or enjoying other hobbies, Fern proves 51 can look fabulous!

Sue Ellen – Cool and light are Sue Ellen's colour characteristics. Cascade shades of blue, crimson, navy and pink are just a few of the many cool tone colours Sue Ellen wears so well. Slightly upper in silhouette, 35 year old Sue Ellen's Clothing Lifestyle is Suburban, stylishly balancing her activities as a wife, mother of three and Pilates instructor.

Sue – Warm in colouring with beautiful red hair, Sue's Cajun category shows warm-toned skin *can* wear black and wear it well. Sue looks stunning in shades of olive, pumpkin, rust and brown. A forty-something manager of cosmetics in a major department store, Sue likes to keep her Metropolitan look current and add stylish flair to her suits. Sue's slender upper silhouette is flattered by details such as collars, turtlenecks, jackets and blazers with lapels.

Elizabeth - Caribbean/Cosmopolitan

Fern - Champagne/Westcoast

Nicole - Crystal/Uptown

Sue - Cajun/Metropolitan

Sue Ellen - Cascade/Suburban

Before

After

Jackie - Chameleon/Metro-Suburban

"Knowing my Current Colours™ and clothing proportions has given me a renewed confidence so valuable for my demanding lifestyle."

Our "before and after" of Jackie demonstrates the importance of knowing your Current Colours™. When Jackie came to have her Style File™ done in the spring of 2003, she was in her late forties and ready for a new look. Colour was the basis for our beginning. Her first characteristic is not warm or cool; it is deep. Jackie is a Chameleon and looks best in deep rich tones. She avoids bright or pale colours and her lighter shades are muted. Obviously she wears black well and also looks good in chocolate brown, plum, raisin and forest green. Lighter shades of dusty rose, pink grapefruit and dusty teal are flattering accent colours. After completing her Style File™, we chose business clothes that were fitting for her high profile consulting job.

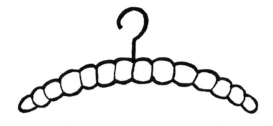

Clutterless

My best buddy says the new trend is feng shui. It seeks to simplify and bring harmony into your life. I, personally, am convinced it is just a fancy term for cleaning your closet. Call it what you like; an organized, clean closet can feel better than a vacation! Like many other habits that are good for us, it seems we tend to procrastinate...

Perhaps you need a little inspiration. Think of all the dollars that are hanging in your closet; clothes that you will never wear again. Here are some suggestions as to who would appreciate them and put your give-aways to good use.

- o A women's transition house
- o A disaster relief organization
- o The Salvation Army
- o Local churches
- o A needy friend

Why *do* we let clothes hang in our closet, taking up room, providing confusion and clutter, when so many people could benefit from our donations? How about making a list of three different places to deliver your cast-offs. As you are eliminating unwanted items, you can choose a specific "home" for each one.

What makes cleaning a closet so difficult? Hmm. What did we mention in **The Many Phases of Eve** chapter – those pesky reasons why we, the "cling-on-tos", choose to battle the forces of our closets each morning.

Might they be…

o   I have a brand new black skirt hanging in my closet. I just need to lose five lbs. to slip into it.

o   I couldn't think of parting with my high school reunion dress. I paid a fortune for it!

o   This sweater was 70% off last spring. Such a bargain! Funny, I can't find anything to wear with it this year.

o   Here's my favorite: if I clean my closet I won't have anything left to wear! (Could there be a contradiction here? Many of those items are not working for you anyway!)

Must I torture you more?

More "sabotage" and women are experts in that department. We orchestrate huge weddings, conferences, family reunions, but a simple wardrobe plan seems out of the realm of possibility. Well, I am sorry to disappoint the highly intelligent, analytical portion of your thought process, but this closet cleaning task is way too easy.

What can you give me – an hour or a weekend?

If you give me a weekend (for an average sized closet), we will sort this out once and for all. If you are eager to begin, and a weekend's worth of time is not an option right now, we can do this an "hour at a time" (H.A.T. approach).

Step 1 – Hangers

Before you begin this rewarding project, I want you to purchase new hangers. Sturdy, plastic hangers will keep your clothing and your closet in tip-top shape. Your clothes hang much better on a proper hanger, thus keeping their shape longer.

Choose clip hangers for skirts and pants, or lay slacks over the rolled cardboard bar of a dry-cleaner's hanger to ensure no creasing. Some plastic hangers will have clips on the bottom bar…

After undressing, I always remove my belt from any skirt, slacks or jeans I am wearing and place it on one of the hooks of a belt hanger. It saves mega-wasted time looking for that certain belt.

A hosiery hanger with clear pouches is perfect for organizing nylons, scarves and/or panties.

Step 2 – Preparation

Make your bed, tidy your room and eliminate ornaments, picture frames, etc. from your dressers. Have ready: garbage bags, storage cartons, notepaper or planner, pen/markers.

Label a bag or carton each for:

o   Your favorite charity

o   A nearly-new shop

o   The garbage bin

Be certain to choose a distinctive bag for the garbage in order to prevent any disasters.

Step 3 - Removal

Remove *all* the items in your closet. If you are doing the H.A.T. approach (hour at a time) remove 20 articles of clothing from your closet.

Now…

Handle each item separately. Place it in one of three piles on your bed.

YES pile   NO pile   MAYBE pile

Step 4 – The YES Pile

The YES pile is the easiest. It consists of all your favorites. And your favorites are favorites for a reason. The fit, style and colour are exactly right for you. There is a stat that says we wear 10% of the clothes in our closet 90% of the time. Surprise, surprise! The 10% are your favorites. The better news is, after reading this book, you will be equipped to always choose favorites. Imagine a 100% wearable wardrobe.

stylefile smartz • If you have items in your YES pile that are needing a coordinating piece to create an outfit, now is the time to write down what you need. A simple reminder can keep you focused the next time you shop.

Step 5 – The NO Pile

Now we need to bear down. These are the items that can be tossed with little regret. Gross errors, sad mistakes – get rid of your absolute NOES. What will you do with these castaways: your favorite charity, a nearly new shop, or simply throw them out? Do so NOW!

DO NOT PUT ANY NOES BACK INTO YOUR CLOSET!!!

Step 6 – Confirmation of Clothing Lifestyle

Before you go any further, I would like you to confirm your Clothing Lifestyle(s) from the **Many Phases of Eve** chapter. Remember, to have a wardrobe that works, you need clothes to suit *this time* in your life – not what worked five years ago or what may work in the future. Choose clothing that meets your everyday needs.

Step 7 – The MAYBE Pile

You have graduated to the most difficult pile. Put on your most ruthless and your toughest attitude. This can be heart wrenching, parting with all those punishing mistakes. You know the clothing dilemmas that:

- o Don't fit
- o Are boring
- o Don't suit
- o Are frumpy
- o Are out-of-style
- o Look too tired

And you are telling me, it is hard to throw these away??? C'mon girl, where's the *stylefile smartz*?

Let's look at each of these reasons for elimination realistically.

Doesn't Fit

I hear your thoughts already; "I'm not buying another black skirt until I can fit into the brand new one hanging in my closet!" (Please see the **How Fitting** chapter.)

Missing valuable essentials in your wardrobe, such as a black skirt, can cause endless, unnecessary frustrations. Could the following scenario be familiar?

You have an unexpected hour to browse your favorite clothing store. Look at that cute black skirt. You try it on. Wow! Does it ever look good. Fits. Comfortable. But, hey you have that new one hanging in your closet. (Remember, the one that doesn't fit.)

And what about that cute little black-and-white sweater? Perfect with the black skirt. What do you end up purchasing? The black-and-white sweater. You get home and guess what, the black skirt *still* doesn't fit. More sabotage, more frustration, more wardrobe confusion, more wasted time.

Here is a suggestion, a new way of handling this needless dilemma...

You are closet cleaning. That new black skirt simply doesn't fit. You put it in your consignment pile. It is better to get a little something for it, and allow someone else to enjoy the skirt while it is still in style. Here's another thought. If and when you do lose weight, the skirt may be outdated and you just might want to celebrate your slimmer shape with a new outfit! Next time you are shopping, you find a dynamite black skirt with a black-and-white sweater. They fit!

Wow! You feel great in this little number! Plus, the black skirt works with many other tops in your wardrobe. Hmm...what a concept. Clothing that actually fits your shape, suits your lifestyle and coordinates with existing pieces in your wardrobe. Looks good, feels great. Just a little too easy!

Don't Suit, Out Of Style, Boring, Frumpy Dilemmas

Can you believe these were actually in your closet??? My nagging tone is definitely in print here!

DO NOT, UNDER ANY CIRCUMSTANCE, PUT THEM BACK IN YOUR CLOSET!!!

Guess what will happen? It will be one of your (how would I politely describe) PMS days. You know, the ones where we subconsciously seem to do everything that makes matters worse. This will be the day you put on a "doesn't fit, doesn't suit, boring, frumpy dilemma" outfit. Uh-oh! Stay out of Mom's way today!

Too Tired

This dilemma is the best one to have; you have enjoyed wearing this item over and over again because the fit, style and colour were perfect for you. Give it a big hug and put it in the garbage. This tired item has been a worker in your wardrobe; it is time for retirement.

Step 8 – Ms. Closet

A job worth doing is worth doing well – your tired-looking closet may need a facelift or complete reconstructive surgery!

She is officially empty. How about a fresh coat of paint to perk her up, and a pretty wallpaper trim to accentuate her lines. Ensure she is well lit so her every item is available for you to coordinate with. (You do not wear what you do not see!)

Take advantage of her shape with one of the many closet organizing systems. Hire a professional or do it yourself, but make the most of her every inch.

 Suggestions such as:

o Replacing a single rod with higher and lower rods. Voila! You have doubled her space.
o Hanging a wardrobe shelf or installing shelving to allow ease and care for sweaters and sweatshirts.
o Shoe racks to keep shoes neat, visible and in good shape.

Ms. Closet l o v e s presenting herself with simplicity – neat, tidy and always efficient. Give her the treatment she deserves and she will reward you for years to come.

Step 9 – The Best Part

Yippee! You are ready to assemble your beautiful closet. Each item should be sorted by now. The NO pile, the tired clothing, the too small items should be in their appropriate bags or boxes.

ONLY THE YESES GO BACK INTO YOUR CLOSET!

If you have items that need mending or dry-cleaning, do so immediately. They are not officially a YES item until those tasks are completed.

Here we go... There are various viewpoints as to how you should arrange the clothing in your closet. One of them is to put all items the same colour together – not my favorite. Often items become lost in the sea of colour and individual pieces are not as visible when you are creatively coordinating. My preference is to gather items together. For example, in my closet from left to right I have:

o   Sleeveless sweaters and tanks
o   Short sleeve fine-knits, blouses
o   Long sleeve blouses, shirts
o   Skirts
o   Slacks
o   Dresses

In my 6 shelving cubicles are:

o   T-shirts
o   Sweatshirts
o   Jeans/khakis
o   Gardening shorts & tops
o   Evening tops
o   Bulky sweaters & cardigans

My cubicles separate my next section where nighties, suits, dresses, evening clothes and coats worn occasionally are hung. I also have a bureau in my dressing room for lingerie, workout gear, bathing suits, shorts and tights.

Unless a suit is a certain colour or distinctive fabric, separate your jackets from your skirts and slacks – you may find they will nicely coordinate with other pieces in your wardrobe.

You are finished! An organized closet is a wonderful accomplishment. The freedom from clutter will allow you a fresh, energizing start to each new day.

Once you have completed a closet overhaul, it usually takes a few hours semi-annually to keep it in order. At the beginning of each fashion season (spring/summer and fall/winter), tidy, re-organize and keep your closet clutterless.

Spending two days per year on your closet will reward you with 363 clutterless days – now *that's* a return on your investment!

The Early Bird Is The Best Dressed Chick

How do I say this nicely?

You have been brainwashed. Thinking that you are a smart shopper and actually shopping smart are two very distinct mind-sets.

Women have become pawns in the "retail sale game". In fact, this erroneous mentality saves little, wastes money and confuses wardrobes.

Do I have your attention? Then let the de-programming begin.

It is well noted that women have a propensity when it comes to the subject matter of shopping. But beware…our natural abilities must be harnessed with skilled techniques or…

Or what! We-see-that-red-sale-sign-which-in-turn-increases-our-heart-rate-which-in-turn-totally-masks-any-sign-of-common-sense-from-our-supposed-intelligent-brainmatter-now-non-functioning-due-to-rapidly-pumping-blood-that-has-completely-taken-over-and - s a y s ,

"WE HAVE TO HAVE THAT BARGAIN!"

Now, where was I?

Most accomplished skills begin with an elementary understanding of basics. Practice and implementation of the basics increase ease and proficiency in the specific skill. The old saying practice makes perfect yet again proves itself.

Hoping this topic has been introduced with eloquence and intelligence, I really want you to get this!

Shopping *is* a skill. Learn, baby, learn and stop feeding that inferno with your hard-earned dollars.

Seven Savvies of Shopping Smartz

$hopping $avvy 1

Knowing your Clothing Lifestyles is the basis of a successful wardrobe. Remember, you do not need lots of clothes; but you do need the clothes to suit your current activities. What styles do you reach for each and every day to compliment your lifestyle?

If you need to re-read **The Many Phases of Eve**, do so now. Be realistic and confirm your Clothing Lifestyles.

$hopping $avvy 2

Shop at the *beginning* of each fashion season. (The two major fashion seasons are: spring/summer and fall/winter.) New fads, trends and colours are introduced at the beginning of these two fashion seasons, which sets the mood for current styles.

Depending upon your budget, purchase at least one *complete* outfit right down to hose, shoes and accessories. The savvy shopper will *happily* pay full price for this outfit because:

o The beginning of the fashion season allows her full range of sizes, colours and styles to choose from
o This complete outfit is always ready, set to go
o As sales come along, she can wisely choose what will compliment her new outfit(s)
o She looks, feels and *is* up-to-date

She will enjoy wearing this outfit so much, the cost-per-wear analysis will more than pay for itself, (as opposed to some bargain worn only once or twice – it is far too costly to shop that way).

$hopping $avvy 3

Always complete each outfit over a short period of time. I have another story for you.

I was working as the fashion consultant for a department store in Victoria several years ago. While returning some items to the racks one day, a shopper approached me with bag in hand. "I just wanted you to know this blouse I am carrying is my own. Look at this label," she exclaimed, "I found it last week at a second hand store for five bucks! Can you believe it? Someone must have paid a fortune for this! I am hoping you can help me." She continued, "I have been all over town for the past week trying to find a pair of slacks or a skirt that might coordinate with it. What can you show me?"

The customer was correct. Someone did pay dearly for that blouse – *10 years ago*. The multi-colours, fabric and shape of the garment were dated. It was no surprise to me she could not find anything suitable. However, I did find a beautiful pair of slacks that could work with her proud purchase. The cost of the slacks was $145.00 (and remember this was several years ago).

"Oh, they look great together – I'll take them!"

"Do you have other tops that will work with your new slacks?" I earnestly asked.

"Not really," she replied, "but these slacks are just what I need for this designer blouse."

She purchased them. Unfortunately, the top still looked out of style. Also, if you totalled the number of hours she spent shopping for those pants, that outfit was VERY COSTLY, another example of putting good money to bad use. The wiser choice would have taken the same $150 to purchase a current outfit suiting her silhouette and Clothing Lifestyle.

Always complete your ensemble within a month. It is no coincidence that tints and shades from previous years are difficult to match in any new fashion season. If turquoise is in style, for example, similar hues will also be found in many of your favorite stores enabling you to mix and match successfully. Waiting until next year to purchase an item you hope will coordinate with the turquoise, may leave you frustrated, as the "new" shade may now be bright aqua. More than likely the bright aqua will not be compatible with last year's turquoise.

No matter what the discount, do not succumb to odd pieces on year-end clearances or the above scenario could be yours!

$hopping $avvy 4

Sometimes everything about an outfit is just right – 10 out of 10. If you try on a "10", *do not* leave it in the store. How many times have you tried on the perfect outfit and thought you would wait until it comes on sale or you simply do not need it right now?

Shall I tell you what happens next? You think about that great outfit, how good you looked in it, how often you could wear it. So…a couple of weeks later you go back to purchase it and IT'S GONE! Frustration, time wasted and your "10" is now working for someone else's wardrobe.

Think of the many times you go shopping and nothing seems to work; the few times you *do* find an outfit you fall in love with, don't go home without it!

$hopping $avvy 5

Purchase less and purchase better quality. Although this is no new revelation, many women do not even consider looking at a higher price point for their clothing. I do understand the rationale. We are women. We are the givers that take care of everyone else, leaving ourselves last on the list. There are the kids, the house, the groceries, etc. etc. Make all the lists you like; you are still fooling yourself. Your best bargain may be your most expensive purchase. I am going to illustrate some basic math to persuade you, but it will not have nearly the impact that buying your first piece of *quality* clothing will.

How well I remember my image instructor drilling this concept deep into my thought process some 20 years ago. I came home and purchased a black wool skirt and black wool slacks. I had never paid $100 (and should I remind you again, this was 20 years ago) for a piece of clothing in my life. I had just shelled out $200 for two items. I can honestly say, when I left the store, I had to find a bench to sit down. What had I just done? I had never spent that amount…or had I? (I totalled my cheque book and visa bill for a period of 12 months and was amazed at the sum of my "odd, little, inexpensive" purchases.) Those were the best basics I had ever purchased. They fit well, looked smart and worked with a variety of sweaters, blouses and blazers. I wore those items for the next three fall/winter fashion seasons until the cost per wear proved I owed *them* money.

Let's take a look.

o Black wool slacks - $100
o Worn on average - 3 times per week
o Fall/winter fashion season weeks for my particular climate – 26 weeks
o Life of slacks – 3 fall/winter fashion seasons
o Number of times worn - 234
o Cost per wear - $.43

An inexpensive pair of slacks at $40 is hard-pressed to survive a month and still look decent. Worn 3 times per week, those slacks cost $3.33 per wear. I cannot afford to shop like that. Can you?

I have a saying that has probably been said many times before, "When you put on your clothes, you put on an attitude." Here is how a "to-die-for" outfit translates into a "you-are-so-worth-it" attitude:

You look in the mirror; the outfit looks fabulous…

It fits. It drapes and hangs well. There is an understated elegance…

You are suddenly standing straighter…

You're smiling…

Oooo you look great!

You could wow the boardroom in this…

The colour is so good on you…

You are imagining all the possibilities while wearing this…

Your grin is wider. You are quietly giggling

You turn around and look back in the mirror…

Looks terrific…

Good thing the change room is a good size…

You have a little strut thing happening…

You toss your hair; tilt your head.

That's it,

YOU ARE TAKING IT!

It's the big day, important meeting, put on your *fave*. Hmm, every time you wear this, and you wear it so much,

You have a fabulous day.

Coincidence?

You tell me.

$hopping $avvy 6

As stated in the **Figure It Out** chapter, "we dress bodies we know little about." Feeling frustrated because a great outfit on a mannequin does not look the same on your shape, is absurd. Follow the chapter carefully to determine your silhouette and proportions.

And don't forget (or ignore), 90% of women need alterations. Clothing comes in a standard sizing; women's bodies do not. Alterations have been the missing ingredient to great-fitting wardrobes.

I had a new client recently who looked absolutely flabbergasted when I explained that her needed alteration was taking in her waistbands. She looked at me and said, "I have no problem hemming my sleeves and my slacks, but I never thought to alter my waistbands. This has been an area of sheer frustration for me. How wonderful – but, oh, how simple!"

$hopping $avvy 7

Know your Current Colours™ and update them every fashion season.

Colour is free! An outfit has to come in one colour or another – why not one that is personally flattering to you? Break out of the old "colour box" and learn the new up-to-date methods that make colour analysis an essential element of shopping smartz. (See **Current Colours™** chapter.)

What a revelation – a clean closet and shopping savvy! I know, I know, you just can't wait to get to the mall! Hang on, you have a little more stylefile smartz to tuck under your belt...

Essentials

Every wardrobe needs some basics. The Style File™ likes to call them essentials. These are the staples in your wardrobe that mix and match and take you most places you need to go on a day-to-day basis.

There are a few key pieces that are part of every successful wardrobe. If you are ever shopping and you see one of the following, but think you do not need it right now, think again. These are the purchases you will always appreciate.

A Suit

Whether a beautiful slack suit or a skirted suit, this dynamic duo will take you so many places. A suit is just as important to a woman's wardrobe as it is to a man's.

An "After 5" Dress

When you find a dress that looks good on you, do not leave it in the store! They say if you have a pretty dress in your closet, you will find a place to wear it!

Coat/Jacket

Depending on your climate, keep this staple dry-cleaned and bagged while out of season.

Appropriate Accessories

Keep belts, shoes and handbags in good condition. Nothing detracts from your style, more than shoddy, worn-out accessories.

While every wardrobe has a few common necessities, your day-to-day staples vary depending on your Clothing Lifestyle(s). A basic wardrobe for you can be entirely different from that of your neighbour. Let us have a look at some key pieces for the various Clothing Lifestyle(s).

 stylefile smartz • Never get stuck in the "box". The following are suggestions, not absolute musts! If you have favorite basics that work well for your wardrobe, ensure these pieces are ready-set-to-go in your closet. Don't forget, keep your "basics" up-to-date in the latest styles and colours, and always, always choose sizing to fit your current shape.

The Style File's™ "Top Ten"

The top ten items for each Clothing Lifestyle may be helpful as you begin to plan your efficient essentials.

My Essentials Shopping List

_____

_____

_____

_____

_____

_____

_____

_____

_____

Metropolitan

Metropolitans require a larger wardrobe than most. It is imperative for Ms. Metro to portray her corporate lifestyle in a classy and professional manner.

Metropolitan suggestions:

o Trench coat

o Multi-purpose blazer

o Skirted suit

o Pant suit

o Dress slacks in dark neutral

o Skirt

o Fine-knit tops

o Blouses

o Leather handbag/tote/briefcase

o Leather pumps

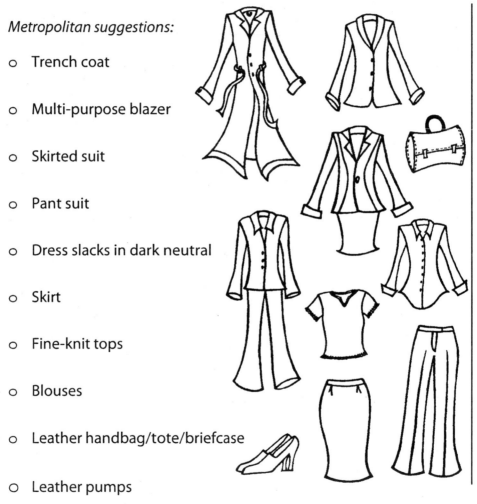

Westcoast

For many women, Westcoast is as dressed up as they need to be for this time in their life. For Metropolitans, often it is as dressed down as they prefer.

Westcoast suggestions:

o   Blazer

o   Cardigan

o   Fine-knit top

o   Shirt/blouse (light neutral)

o   Casually smart slacks

o   Khakis

o   Dress slacks

o   Skirt

o   Leather flats

o   Casually smart handbag

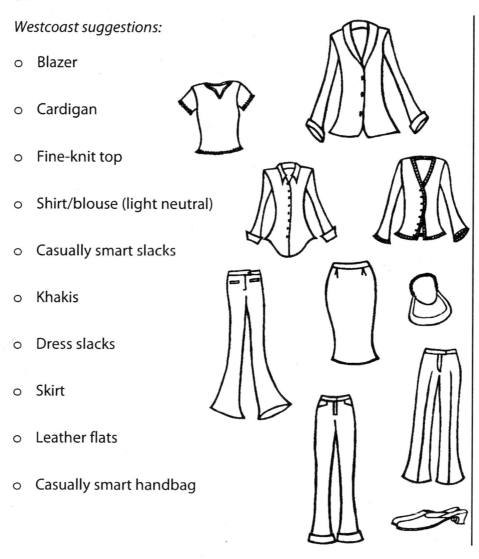

Suburban

Nearly every lifestyle incorporates a Suburban look. Whether you are a full time mom, retired businesswoman or enoy playing on the weekend, the biggest complaint of a casual lifestyle is it becomes *too* casual. Remember casual does NOT mean sloppy. Put some pizzazz in your casual wardrobe and watch your confidence grow.

Suburban suggestions:

o   A great pair of jeans

o   Cotton khakis

o   Casual blazer/jacket

o   Cardigan

o   Light neutral shirt

o   Light neutral knit top

o   Pullover/sweatshirt

o   Casual skirt

o   Loafers

o   Tote/bag

Cosmopolitan

You can always notice a cosmopolitan woman, with that feminine allure and grace. She loves any excuse for dressing up and chooses soft, swishy fabrics. Her tops will be favorites if they have ribbon, crochet or lace trim. Stiff denim is her least favorite, so if Ms. Cosmo should have a need for jeans, tencel denim would be her fabric of choice.

Cosmo suggestions:

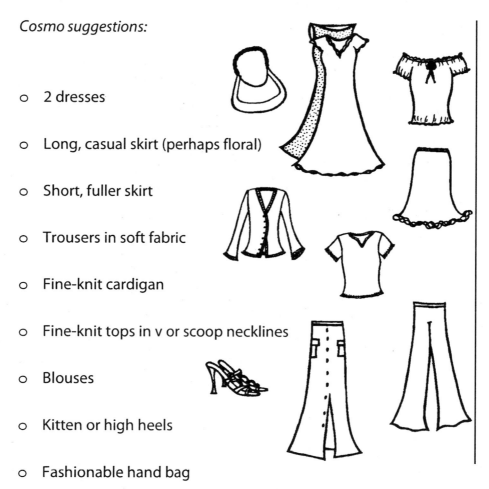

o   2 dresses

o   Long, casual skirt (perhaps floral)

o   Short, fuller skirt

o   Trousers in soft fabric

o   Fine-knit cardigan

o   Fine-knit tops in v or scoop necklines

o   Blouses

o   Kitten or high heels

o   Fashionable hand bag

Uptown

This lifestyle needs no list or suggestions. If I were to list 10 items they would be out-of-date and boring to Mz. Uptown by the time this book was in print. Outrageous, off-the-runway styles, mixing patterns and colours; she can put it together with an enviable flair.

If you have completed your closet clean, you will easily see the suitable yeses you have left to work with. After checking your Clothing Lifestyle(s) Top Ten, write down the missing essentials you need to help coordinate your wardrobe.

Keep your options open while you are shopping, but do refer to your list. It certainly helps to keep you on track of your clothing needs, eliminating the "wow-it-was-such-a-good-buy" purchase you usually come home with.

It's a plan, Fran – stick to it!

Stages Of Ages

It just happens. No rhyme, no reason, no special birthday, no particular time of the year. It just happens. You look in the mirror and something is different, not quite right. The tired excuse is wearing thin. The bathroom lighting is the same as it has always been.

And then your inner mirror reflects the reality that your mirror, mirror on the wall has been trying to tell you. (Oh that inner mirror. It's so...so...brutally honest.) The naked truth is YOU'RE...GETTING... OLDER.

Yes, you are. But before the panic sets in, I would like you to consider an astonishing fact – that's what happens to humans! OK? Finished with the doom and gloom? Good, because I have a challenge for you. This three part challenge will shatter your inner mirror and have your mirror,

mirror on the wall asking a whole new set of questions. Forget the "fairest"; who is this sexy mama!

Part I

The first part of the challenge is the most important. In fact, it is the essence of The Style File™. Attitude. And attitude is *everything!*

I'm going to ask you to grab a piece of paper and a pen. Please do not read any further until you do this. On your piece of paper I want you to list three figure faults. Yes…only three. (This little experiment only works by following the steps.) Finished with your list? Now, list three positive physical attributes. Not that you are a great cook or a super tennis player – three positive, physical attributes. Honestly, did you have more difficulty listing three positives over three negatives?

I have been doing this survey for the past 20 years and in each women's group, 90% quickly list the negatives. Every seminar, someone *always* asks, "only three"? When I ask for the positives, there is an initial bewildering silence.

We are so busy giving attention to the few things we do *not* like about ourselves, that we fail to recognize all our positives! All the details we do not complain about are positives! Average size foot, graceful shoulders, medium length neck.

So what's the big deal about an average size foot? Ask the woman with size 5AA or size 11D, which makes her shoe shopping and fitting a nightmare. A medium length neck? Ask the woman with a very short neck and she will tell you necklines are always an issue.

We *all* have our little negative list, but an optimistic attitude helps you handle the list and discover how to flaunt the positives. The result – an original, one-of-a-kind – you! Judy Garland once said, "Always be a 1st rate version of yourself, never a 2nd rate version of someone else." Wow!

Do you know what really attracts people to others – the captivating, magnetic quality that everyone can own? Confidence! The confidence that marries the inner attitude with the outer appearance; the confidence that says I'm happy in my own skin, I know where I'm going and what I am all about.

Part II

I have to disagree with the old saying, "a change is as good as a rest". Change is w *a y* better than a rest. Nothing stays the same, so why should we? Be open to change. Embrace it! It is the spice of life!

When a woman comes for her Style File™, more often than not there is a subconscious mind-set that says, "Yes, I have come for a change – but please keep everything the same." Ha! We get into such a rut, we are almost fearful to climb out!

Mary came to have her Style File™ done. She was middle age, petite, lovely gray hair and a very shapely figure. She was wearing a skirt and a "tired" white blouse. It had a dainty collar and was fully buttoned up. As we became comfortable discussing her past, it became evident she was stuck in the 80's. Back then, women were forging their way into a male-dominated work force. Women's professional dress was tailored with imposing shoulder pads in their notched lapel blazers, classic blouses (buttoned to the top) and always completed with a skirt. Yes, times had changed.

Mary had donned the stiff blazer, but was unsure how to put her new look together. She now is a job coach. Her clothes need to speak "professional" but also approachable and up-to-date. We discussed the messages and signals our clothing sends to others. Buttoned-up blazers and blouses send stiff signals of inaccessibility.

I began by asking her to open her top button. You cannot imagine how difficult it was for Mary to undo that button! It was totally out of her comfort zone. At the end of her Style File™, she asked, "can I do up my button now?"

"Of course you can," I replied. "Thanks for being a good sport and trying it out."

Our next session was a shopping trip. Mary was preparing for an international conference and needed some clothes that said capable, confident and classy. We found her a periwinkle pantsuit with a silk, knit top. She looked fabulous.

I saw Mary in the mall about a month later. "I received so many compliments. I *love* my new look! By the way," she added, "I never do up that top button anymore. Been there, done that, don't want the shirt."

Sometimes we just need permission to change, permission to climb out of the rut, and permission to continue the amazing discovery process of who we are and what we can become.

Part III

A positive attitude and being open to change naturally evolves into the third part of your challenge. Approach each new stage of your life with zest and enthusiasm. Look where you have come from, and the opportunities that lie ahead. Your style should be "in the now". Ban those old-fashioned habits and looks, and make the most of this new stage in your life.

Guess what? This stage in your life will never come again. In 10 years you will be wishing you were this age once more, so get going girl! Perhaps it is time for a different hairstyle or a spicy new shade of colour. Experimenting with warmer hues of make-up can soften a mature complexion. And, definitely, updating your colours each fashion season with the Current Colours™ system, enhances skin tones that are forever changing. Shorten your skirts or lengthen your jackets. Find out what is "in" and how you can energize your wardrobe with a fresh fad or two. You will be so rejuvenated with a new look that this energy will spill over into other aspects of your life as well!

The Final Equation:

(attitude + age) x (style + confidence) = The Look!

The Look on the outside that reflects one healthy, happy person on the inside! It's a stylefileism, "If you look good, you feel good, and if you feel good, you *are* good!"

Puttin' On The Ritz

Have you ever read the enticing caption on a fashion magazine cover that says, "2 inches taller in 30 seconds!"? Wow! I'm buying that mag. You turn to page 95 to discover this amazing miracle and what does it show – a simple exercise in posture. Simple, yes, but instantly uplifting and visually powerful.

Putting on good posture is worth far more than putting on an expensive outfit. Oh – I saw that! The mere mention of the word posture and you are suddenly sitting or standing straighter.

More than likely, your youthful posture has disappeared, and…exactly when was it that the slouch strolled through the door and made herself at home? Her chain reaction shrunk your silhouette and destroyed that sexy strut. Hey, girlfriend – send the slouch packing. You are an easy exercise away from a proud posture you won't want to leave home without!

Catch yourself looking in a full-length mirror when you are unprepared and this is what you may see. The chin has tilted downward forcing the head and neck to sink into the shoulders – the chain reaction begins. The shoulders cave in, reducing those oh-so-precious-inches-where-we-want-them. (We actually *do that* to ourselves?) The stomach protrudes more than necessary and the feet become filled with concrete-like matter that disables you from picking them up properly. Voila – the slouch.

OK. Enough is enough. Ready?

Stand up straight. Take a deep breath and roll your shoulders in a full circle beginning with a forward motion, then heading upward toward the ears. Do this entire motion slowly while consciously thinking of each point mentioned. Feel your shoulders trying to reach your ears, then slowly complete the circle, pressing the shoulders backward to their final resting position.

Ensure your head is squarely on your shoulders. (Envision an invisible string on top of your head attached to the ceiling.) The chin should *not* be up in the air, nor tilted down, but facing front. It should feel like someone is placing their hands on your shoulders and firmly pressing down. You should also see and feel the neck lengthening. Let your arms naturally fall at your side. Careful – there is a tendency to stiffen the arms while thinking of all these new positions!

Inhale again and repeat:

- o Circular motion forward
- o Shoulders reaching the ears
- o Complete circular motion
- o Head straight
- o Chin forward

Well that takes care of the top half of our body, let's put the bottom half in sync. Stand with your feet slightly apart. As you exhale from your deep breath and shoulder circle, pelvic tilt. (For those who do not know what a pelvic tilt is, lift the hips forward and tighten the buttocks; gently squeeze as if you were holding a penny between your cheeks.) Now your silhouette is in line.

What a difference! This may feel foreign for many of you, but if you apply the old practice-makes-perfect rule (practising for 10 minutes a day, for 30 consecutive days), your new posture will be as natural as your smile. What have you got to lose?

Face The Facts

Your skin has to last a lifetime. There is no time like *right now* to begin, or improve, caring for this precious treasure. Developing and maintaining a scrupulous skin care routine, will be one of a woman's best-rewarded disciplines.

Never ignore or take your skin for granted. Approximately 80% of aging is a result of environmental factors over which you *do* have control. Improper cleansing, poor diet, insufficient sleep, sun damage, smoking, alcohol and drugs will show on your skin long before your age catches up.

Experiment with different skin care lines and discover what products are most beneficial to your particular skin type. I was fortunate to find a skin care line in my mid 20's, which not only cleared up my spotty skin, but has also kept it glowing and healthy ever since. Remember…what you put on your skin does not topically remain there – it is absorbed into the body. Know your cosmetics and their contents and do not be fooled by a "name".

Is your skin dry, oily or a combination? Keep up-to-date with your skin type; just like the rest of you, it is forever changing. You may find the best product on the market, but if it is for oily skin and yours is dry, it will *not* be correct for you. Most skin care companies train their consultants well, so spend some time asking questions and testing products.

Your Skin's Fitness Program

- o The basic three + one
- o Cleanse, tone & moisturize
- o Morning & evening

Oh, c'mon…isn't that just a ploy to have us purchase products we really don't need?

You decide.

Cleanse

While you are sleeping oils, sweat and toxins are released from your pores. The good news: the oils lubricate and protect the skin while the sweat helps to neutralize the oils. The bad news: if left on the skin the oils will trap dirt and bacteria and cause the pores to become clogged.

Cleansing your skin in the morning ensures your pores remain as clean as possible.

In the evening it is imperative that the dust and dirt of everyday living be removed. Some of you are blessed with incredible skin that appears to require little attention, but beware…your day of reckoning will come. What is that saying? For every night you go to bed without removing your make up, your skin ages seven days!

Tone

Your skin's natural pH balance is 4.5 – 6. It is no coincidence it is slightly acidic in nature. Germs cannot live in an acidic base, but thrive in an alkaline base. Guess what condition cleansers and soaps leave on your skin – *oh* ya – alkaline. A toner returns the skin to its natural pH balance. If you omit this step, it takes nature approximately three to six hours to return the skin to a slightly acidic base. Hmm…who are you working for – the health of your skin or the health of the germs?

stylefile smartz • A toner or astringent should never bite or sting. If it does, this often means there is alcohol in the product and that can be disturbing to the moisture level of your skin - even oily skin.

Moisturize

Even oily skin needs moisture. I will do the broken record thing and remind you to choose a product that will work WITH your skin type. If you use a product for dry skin on oily skin, the product will "sit" on the surface and feel greasy. At the opposite end of the scale, if your skin is constantly feeling taut and tight, you may need to choose a different moisturizer to nourish your dry skin.

The best analogy to encourage you to moisturize is the plum and the prune. If you leave the plum in the sun it shrivels to a prune. Open the prune and it is still "oily". It is the lack of moisture that causes the cells to collapse and shrivel. Get the picture???

+ One

Huh? + One? Well, that is something new. Actually it is not so new, but grouping it into the basic three *is*. I am sure you can guess what I am about to preach – the necessity of daily SUNSCREEN. I use a moisturizer with an SPF 18 and apply liberally to my face and neck. Whether a moisturizer or a separate product, apply sunscreen before you put on foundation. This step is not an option; it is a must.

Now really…3 + 1 twice a day is not asking much for a life-long return.

Special Attention

Once or twice a week, depending on your skin type, a gentle exfoliant and masque will help slough off dead skin cells and deep cleanse the pores.

Your skin will benefit from any and all the attention you choose to give it. And…never underestimate the importance of your esthetician. We in North America are much slower than our European counterparts when it comes to regular visits to an esthetician. While North American women often view this treatment as a luxury, Europeans protect their skin with routine facials, knowing the life-long benefit of this essential part of their beauty regime.

Make-up Application

Okay, I must say, you have been patient. You are really just waiting to discover the deep exotic mysteries of make-up application. Right? Well I don't know about the deep exotic part, but I do know, building five or ten minutes into your morning routine for some easy, *stylefile* make-up *smartz*, is a vital part of your personal style.

I do not believe make-up should be something you "put on", but rather, it should enhance your natural features. Beautiful, young skin needs little attention, but did you know that by the time you have reached 25 your natural glow begins to fade?

Foundation

A little help with foundation goes a l o n g way. Gone are the days when foundations clogged the pores and left you with an orange ring around the face. A suitable foundation evens out the skin tone, minimizes the redness of rosaeca and blends with your natural colouring. Too light a shade leaves you looking pale and unhealthy; too dark and the proverbial ring around the face lets the world know your eye sight and/or bathroom lighting is in dire need of help!

I prefer a liquid foundation, which leaves the skin with a dewy finish. If you are unusually oily, try a powder or an oil-free liquid formula.

Always use a sponge when blending your foundation. My preference is a sea-sponge, although many choose the latex triangle. This amazing make-up tool not only blends your foundation easily and naturally, it avoids your fingers touching and pulling at your face.

Whether golfing or gardening, if you spend time outdoors, chances are you need to darken your foundation during the warm-weather months.

Blush

Please treat yourself to a full, natural blush brush. Trying to apply blush powder with a skinny, narrow brush will leave your cheeks in streaks! A quality blush brush disperses the powder so you are free to "blush" with a healthy looking glow. Dust your brush diagonally on your cheek, between the top of the ear and the outer corner of your actual eye, blushing slightly under the cheekbone.

 stylefile smartz • As you age your make-up tones often become warmer. If pink or rose blush begins to "sit" on the skin, it may be time to consider a tawnier shade.

Eyes

Because eyes come in thousands of shapes, it is difficult to state a few general guidelines. I will encourage you, however, to carefully read the eye basics and determine which methods most enhance your shape.

I do believe eyes are the mirror of the soul and along with your smile these powerful expressions of non-verbal communication instantly reveal much about who you are.

Nothing will date you faster than old-fashioned eye make-up! Liner and shadow application is always changing and it is important to keep up with the trends. If you have been wearing the same liner and shadows for several years – it's time for a change!!!

Eye Basics

Before you begin applying your <u>eye shadow</u>, examine the natural colouring on your eyelids. Many people have hues of purple, green or brown on their lids. If so, be certain to even out your eyelid with a bit of foundation or lighter shadow, much the same as evening out your skin tone with foundation.

I vividly remember a new client coming in for her Style File™. When we began doing Sarah's make-up, I did the basic cleanse, tone and moisturize, then handed her a cotton pad to remove her eye make-up. She looked a little puzzled and asked what she should do with this. "I would like you to remove your eye make-up," I responded, looking just as puzzled.

"Oh, I don't have any on," Sarah replied.

Now, quietly thinking I have lost it, I looked a little closer. Her perfectly contoured brown "shadow" on the brow bone and eyelid was actually her natural colouring.

Do you want a hint as to what happened next? Let me give you a few more of the puzzle pieces. Her skin was a cool tone and her hair was a beautiful silver gray. "I always feel I look tired," Sarah sighed, "no matter how much blush I put on."

This was too much fun and way too easy! Blush had nothing to do with the issue. We dabbed a little foundation over the eye area, then applied a light pearl gray on the lid and a granite contour. It was magical! Sarah's entire face lit up. All her cool tone colouring needed was to remove the natural brown shading on her eye. She looked absolutely radiant.

The usual rule of thumb for shadow application is light on the lid and dark on the orbital bone. Fine if you have a small to normal lid like Sarah, but if your lid is prominent and you apply light shadow you only exaggerate the proportion. Choose a neutral shadow on the lid and watch how the eye becomes accentuated.

Contouring with a darker shadow on the orbital bone enhances most eye shapes. Choose tones to compliment your colouring.

 stylefile smartz • Use the magic of contour for hooded eyelids. On one eye, use a matte shadow and stop the contour line on the orbital bone just above the outside corner of your eye. Blend well. On the other eye, continue the contour to the base of the orbital bone right beside the outside edge of the eye. Notice the difference! Ending the contour shadow above the outside corner of the eye visually "lifts" while extending the shadow to the base draws the shape of the eye downward.

<u>Eye liner</u> dramatically defines the eye. As you reach your forties and fifties, choose a pewter or brown in place of black liner. The look becomes softer and more flattering. If you are still lining the bottom of your eyes only, like you did in the early 90's, climb out of the time warp and pay attention to the current trends.

A well-shaped <u>eyebrow</u> frames the eye more than you realize. A visit to your esthetician for this simple and inexpensive procedure will be well worth it.

 stylefile smartz • Never "draw" with an eyebrow pencil. Instead, use small, shading strokes backwards from the outside to inside of the brow. Complete with an eyebrow brush following the natural growth of the brow. The pencil shading blends into your natural brow – it's a pretty finish.

Last, but most importantly, is <u>mascara</u>. For 90% of women, this is as much a part of your morning routine as brushing your teeth. What a difference! Often eyelashes are dyed to eliminate this step and achieve the same look. Don't forget, if your colouring is extremely light try brown mascara. It will take away the harsh look of black mascara for many blonde, fair-skinned women.

Here is a colour fact for make-up and clothing: light colours bring forward and dark colours recede. This definitely applies to <u>lipstick</u>. If you have thinner lips, use a lighter colour to make lips appear larger. If you have fuller lips, you will find darker, matte shades are more appealing than glossy lipsticks.

Lip liner can be used for an evening look, but becomes a basic when we reach those mid years. Your lip liner should be the colour of your lips when wet. We all know what too dark a liner does…

Overwhelmed? You shouldn't be. A quick recap and we have:

Skin Care

- o   3 + 1 – twice a day

- o   Cleanse… Tone… Moisturize

- o   Sunscreen under make-up

Make-up

Foundation… Blush… Eyes… Lips

Hey, you are ready set for each and every day!

(Should I nag, "practice makes perfect?"…nah I wouldn't do that)

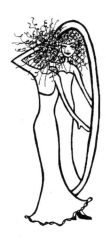

What's Wrong With This Picture?

How do I stress the importance of this small chapter? All the Style File™ know-how becomes redundant if this element of your style is neglected. To say that your hair is your "crowning glory" is an understatement!

One of your most important style gurus is your hair stylist. If you have not found *your* stylist as yet, make it a priority. One of the easiest ways to find a great hair stylist is to simply ask someone whose hairstyle you love. "Where do your get your hair done?" can solve such a dilemma in an instant.

The Style File's™ hair stylist, Tony Sabine, is adamant about the first step in a stylist/client relationship. "Be aware, the stylist should *always* sit you down for a five or ten minute consultation before anything else.

This allows him/her to analyze your hair and face shape to get to know what you are looking for and can handle in a hairstyle."

He goes on to say, "If you are taken from the waiting lounge to the sink, you may want to think twice about choosing that particular stylist."

If you have had the same "do" for the past several years, it is *so* time for a change, Tina. What do you have to lose? Unfortunately, I still hear women commenting on leaving their hair long (and often unstyled) because that is the way their husbands like it. I am not even going to go there, other than repeating "a change is way better than a rest" (and I am talking hairstyles here). Your look will only be improved. Just because you are changing your hairstyle does not mean you need to go short or bald or purple! Not only are there so many fabulous, easy styles nowadays, but also products and tools to help you get the look you want.

How excited was I when Tony introduced me to my favorite brand of gel! Wash, towel dry, quick brush, tong a few stubborn areas and finger-gel throughout my hair and literally "set" my hair with my fingers. Yippee! Quick and easy, yes, but the true maintenance for *my* hairstyle is the fact that I have my short hair cut every two and a half to three weeks.

I know we all want hair we cannot have. I would have given most anything to have long, silky, beautiful hair, but it was not meant to be. I looked "old" at eleven when my thick, straight hair was growing long.

And of course, when I was only six, my older brother would constantly tease me that pretty girls could copy the T.V. commercial – the one where her lovely long hair moved ever-so-slowly (unbeknownst to me, in slow motion) as she shook her head from side to side – and I could never seem to do that.

Your particular type of hair and shape of face determines what will best suit you and that is what it is all about. I don't need to remind you that the beautiful Halle Berry looks stunning with her short hair.

Style is all about choosing your personal best, and your hairstyle is actually the beginning of developing your personal style.

Your stylist is eagerly waiting to bring you into the 21st century. By the way, if your stylist has been cutting your hair the same way for many years, and does not give you new suggestions from time to time, perhaps it is the stylist you need to change before the hairstyle.

So…what does it take to maintain your daily hair routine? My hair needs washing every day, but if your hair is dry, you may find every second day suits you better. Whatever works best, do it. Never try and s t r e t c h that extra day; it is never becoming.

Take pictures of favorite styles to visually let your stylist know what you have in mind. He or she will advise you as to whether your hair can handle the look. Discuss new products, treatments, tools and cuts to determine what will most flatter your hair and your face shape. Learn everything you can about your particular hair: thick/thin, dry/oily, curly/straight.

I am diligent about making time for my haircuts. My suggestion, along with every hair stylist's, is to make your next appointment before you leave the salon. Do you think it is a coincidence that your mood suddenly becomes uplifted after having your hair done?

As in every other element of style, your personal knowledge increases confidence and know-how in choosing everything from clothing to make-up to hairstyles.

Details

Finishing Touches.

I would never go out of the house without my _____. How do you fill in the blank: lipstick, hair done, nail polish, mascara, earrings, make-up? Almost every woman has a particular beauty detail that must be completed before she feels "ready".

Along with your "beauty-musts" however, are the subtleties that characterize a woman's style; the quiet, little details that speak classy and confident. The finer points granted, take a small effort, but undeniably put the "I-can't-help-but-notice-you" strut in your step. Ignorance or avoidance of the details (which curiously happens on our not-so-happy days) instantaneously tarnishes the look *and* the attitude!

How about a quiz to sharpen your finer points awareness?

o   Do you keep your nails well-shaped and filed?

o   Do you ever wear your nail polish chipped?

o   Are your eyebrows plucked and shaped?

o   Are your legs, underarms and bikini line smooth?

o   Do you wear belts with frayed edges or tired buckles?

o   Do you wear shoes that need to be polished or re-heeled?

o   Is your hair colour showing an overdue demarcation line?

o   Is your purse worn and needing replacing?

o   Have you updated your glasses within the last three years?

We are not going to tally up the yeses and noes, and the list is by no means complete, but this exercise is meant to provoke a little action to the issues needing your attention.

"Ay-yai-yai, where do I draw the line?" you ask in frustration. Well let me pointedly re-phrase the question. What finer points would you handle if you were asked out on a special date??? I rest my case…just handle them! If you tend to overlook these appropriate details, "pretend" you are going out on a date once a month. Now honey, you'll be stylin'!

Exercise and Diet

In the 21st century, no self-help book would be complete without the encouragement of exercise and a balanced diet. Thousands of men and women have looked, are looking, and will continue to look for the all-encompassing sentence that would make each and every person responsible for his/her health. We just don't get another body – we need to take care of the one we are given!

Hectic lifestyles often replace wholesome diets with unhealthy substitutes. Combined with the frightening fact we are spending more sedentary time in front of our computer screens, our poor bodies are desperate for much-needed attention!

As with any new routine or goal in your life, begin small and begin realistically. Walking, weights, dancing, gardening – choose an activity or sport of interest to you. We really *do* know that fad diets are more harmful than good; try replacing your coffee and muffin with water and a banana once a day and start from there.

A fit body (*not* a skinny body) builds self-esteem, confidence and a happy outlook. You *can* do it – it is simply your choice.

Knack To Pack

Travel – the mere word evokes thoughts of adventure, fun, romance, and best of all, a time to leave your worries and cares at home.

Just pack up and go. Ahh, how wonderf …

P A C K!!! Oh no – more stress! What to wear? What to take? And of course, how to stuff it in a suitcase without any creasing?

Relax. If you follow the **Knack to Pack** suggestions you will be amazed at your packing proficiency!

So, at the risk of provoking any procrastinating natures, I would like to *strongly suggest* a little preparation. An hour of planning will assist your packing far more than you can imagine.

Step I – Your Suitcase

A functional suitcase is a must. My personal preference is the upright pullman. Wheels, adjustable handles and removable straps are vital for ease and comfort while transporting your luggage.

A practical size for your pullman will depend on the type of travelling you do.

- o Are you packing for business, pleasure, or both?
- o What is the climate of your destination?
- o How long will you be away?
- o Will laundry facilities be available?

Basic questions that eliminate unwelcome surprises when you arrive.

Look for extra compartments and outside zippers. Be sure and get into the habit of keeping certain items in the same compartments; locating them becomes mere routine.

Step II – Necessities

Here's a thought. How nice it is to handle these necessities at least two weeks before departure, rather than a night or two before you leave:

- o Current passport & appropriate I.D.
- o Travel insurance
- o Prescriptions
- o Dry-cleaning & mending

Step III – "The Hanging Basket"

My firefighter husband, Dave, can fix anything. Imaginative, practical and most resourceful, he simply gets the job done. Along with his male perspective, he has his own "language" and it took me awhile to learn its translation. As we were packing for our first big trip, I was scouring the house for my make-up and toiletries bag. "Oh, you mean your hanging basket?" (Of course, he knew exactly where it was.) Hanging basket? A basket full of toiletries that hangs over a rod or hook…hmm makes sense, I guess.

Regardless of what you choose to call it, purchase one. It will become your best friend! I have mine stocked and ready to go at all times. (A great source for favorite products should you unexpectedly run out of something.)

I usually wear out my "hanging basket" every year or year-and-a-half and I replace it immediately. In fact, when we were building our home, I used it all the time.

I choose a larger style with clear, plastic pockets. Every item is kept in the same place so I know precisely which "pocket to pick". It eliminates clutter on the counter and the need to search for counter space in an unfamiliar place. "Hanging baskets" are simply a must!

A word to the wise when packing your toiletries: put your skin care and make-up in small, plastic containers. Be certain to use well-sealed baggies for items that could possibly cause a disastrous leak.

Step IV – Planning

It is March and you are booked on a Caribbean cruise. Lucky you! Cruising is a wonderful way to travel. And when did you say you're going? Next January. For millions living in the Northern Hemisphere, it is bliss to escape this often-dreary, winter month.

Remember my *suggestion* at the beginning of the chapter? You know, the one about a little planning. This is it, honey. This is the step that will not only leave you feeling quite proud of yourself, but will definitely add to the ambiance and excitement of your journey. You will have all spring and summer to purchase your cruise wardrobe for January.

Oh, you're a last minute gal? Uh-huh. Other than a mere spattering of cruise clothes in expensive boutiques at Christmas time, where will you purchase summer attire in the middle of winter? When you have advance time to put your wardrobe together, p l e a s e take advantage of that opportunity. Besides, you are not just planning a cruise wardrobe; you will have next summer's clothing ready, set to go. Plan and choose your clothing related to your travel needs. It is just that simple.

Step V – Preparation
o   Dry-cleaning

o   Washing

o   Mending

o   Trying on to see if it fits

Obvious to some, oblivious to others, these basic details make a huge difference. Unless you have a personal valet in your closet, the items you put away will be in the same condition coming out as they were going in. Check your travel clothing two to three weeks prior to packing to ensure there are no unwelcome surprises.

Step VI – Packing Tips

Put these straightforward packing tips and techniques into practice. Your clothing and your suitcase will love them!

Crease Minimizers

Always hang on to your dry-cleaning bags and tissue paper. Put either/or in between the folds of your clothes to lessen wrinkles. As you pack a couple of pairs of pants, have the top waist portions of each pair placed in opposite ends of the suitcase with the legs crease-to-crease inside the case. Then fold the top waist portion onto the legs on the bottom, the second pair's legs over the top waist and finally the second pair's top waist portion. Each section of the pant acts as a barrier and prevents creasing. If you have just picked up items from the cleaners to go on your trip, do not take them out of their dry-cleaning bags. Pack them as is.

"Rolling" clothing is very efficient for saving space and eliminating wrinkling.

D.W.'s Slider

When you need different styles of clothing for one trip, pack your heavy items on the bottom of the suitcase. Just before you pack your dressy clothes on top, lay a large beach towel over the heavy items. Pack your good clothing on top of the towel. When you reach your destination, simply lift the towel out of the suitcase to reach the lower items. Your careful packing of the top layer remains undisturbed!

☺ And to think a man figured this out!!!

Step VII – Let's Pack

OK. All set? Dry-cleaning bags, smaller plastic bags, tissue and beach towel ready? Let's pack.

First into the suitcase are shoes. I prefer to put them individually in smaller plastic bags. I stuff them with socks, nylons and underwear to prevent any crushing. Pack them at the base of the case.

Next I pack heavier items, usually neatly rolled. If a fabric is delicate, I lay tissue paper, then roll the article with the tissue inside. I lay the slider down (you know, D.W.'s beach towel idea), then pack my better clothing on top, with tissue or in dry-cleaning bags.

Avoid packing wire hangers. Should they somehow get wet, they may rust or mark clothing. If you need to pack hangers, opt for plastic, and make sure they have clips so you can hang slacks or skirts as well.

Keep the mesh, zippered pockets for delicates (i.e. lingerie) and keep the same items in the same pockets. I know, I'm nagging, but you'll thank me for it in the end.

I always keep my "hanging basket", curling iron and one change of clothes in my carry-on to avoid potential disasters should your luggage become misplaced or lost.

If you have any neck, shoulder or back issues a smart "backpack" purse is like an extra arm balanced evenly on your back. My preference for sure! If you are travelling in countries where you may feel unsafe, choose a money belt on the inside of your clothing. Better safe than sorry!

Always pack some type of hat for sun protection and a plastic poncho (that folds into a small square) to prevent a torrential soaking.

When you are packed, double check that your suitcase is labelled and identifiable. I choose metallic wired ribbon, tied to my handles, to easily spot them on the airport's luggage carousel.

It will be no coincidence that your trip will be fuss free, care free and totally enjoyable if you follow this chapter's suggestions.

I am sure everyone has a special tip that works well. Share your suggestions with an email to: book@stylefilesystem.com. We will post some of them on The Style File™ website at www.stylefilesystem.com.

On A Personal Note

Whew! Who knew a woman's style was so carefully put together and who knew it could be so much fun!

Unlocking the secrets of a woman's style with such a positive approach provides a very gratifying career! But…encouragement works both ways…

As with each and every life, situations and struggles lead us down many different paths: for me the road always led back to my passion for The Style File™. Just when I thought the tough times were too tough, someone would *always* phone and say how The Style File™ has changed their life. Thank you to each and every woman who took the time and effort to make that call; you are the reason this book is in print. That is the power of encouragement.

Now I have a challenge for you. I would like you to take a picture of yourself at this time. When you have put every chapter of Style File™ Know-How into practice, putting all the puzzle pieces together, take another picture. Treat yourself to a double frame and proudly display it where you will look at it everyday. Know how good it *feels* to look your best. My mantra is: when you look good, you feel good, when you feel good you *are* good. Now...go and be great! There is no one else quite like you.

About The Author

Shelley Brown-Williams has been hooked on the high of helping women look their best since 1983. Early in her career, Shelley trained with Vogue Color Consultants and the London Image Institute.

From personal consultations to fashion shows and seminars, Shelley has inspired thousands of women with her highly personable approach to style.

"Style File™ Know-How" is a result of Shelley's passion to share The Style File™ Image Consulting System with each and every woman.

Shelley resides in beautiful Victoria, British Columbia, Canada with her husband Dave and her shih tzu McBeal.

Jan. clean → website week 1 → 4.

ISBN 141201266-X

9 781412 012669